WAR

OPPOSING VIEWPOINTS®

OTHER BOOKS OF RELATED INTEREST

OPPOSING VIEWPOINTS SERIES

American Foreign Policy
America's Defense
The Breakup of the Soviet Union
Central America
Eastern Europe
Global Resources
Global Warming
Human Nature
Human Rights
Islam
The New World Order
The Third World
The War on Drugs
Weapons of Mass Destruction

CURRENT CONTROVERSIES SERIES

Hunger
Interventionism
Nationalism and Ethnic Conflict
Urban Terrorism

AT ISSUE SERIES

Ethnic Conflict
The United Nations

WAR

OPPOSING VIEWPOINTS®

Tamara L. Roleff, *Book Editor*

David L. Bender, *Publisher*
Bruno Leone, *Executive Editor*
Bonnie Szumski, *Editorial Director*
David M. Haugen, *Managing Editor*

OPPOSING
VIEWPOINTS®
SERIES

Greenhaven Press, Inc., San Diego, California

Cover photo: Lau Van der Stockt
Map by Lineworks, Inc.

Library of Congress Cataloging-in-Publication Data

War : opposing viewpoints / book editor, Tamara L. Roleff.
    p.   cm. — (Opposing viewpoints series)
    Includes bibliographical references and index.
    ISBN 0-7377-0061-0 (lib. : alk. paper). —
ISBN 0-7377-0060-2 (pbk. : alk. paper)
    1. War. 2. Intervention (International law). 3. United States—
Foreign relations. 4. United States—Military policy. 5. International
police. 6. Security, International. I. Roleff, Tamara L., 1959–   .
II. Series: Opposing viewpoints series (Unnumbered)
U21.2.W377 1999
355.02—dc21   98-32019
                                                            CIP

Greenhaven Press, Inc., P.O. Box 289009
San Diego, CA 92198-9009

"CONGRESS SHALL MAKE NO LAW...ABRIDGING THE FREEDOM OF SPEECH, OR OF THE PRESS."

First Amendment to the U.S. Constitution

The basic foundation of our democracy is the First Amendment guarantee of freedom of expression. The Opposing Viewpoints Series is dedicated to the concept of this basic freedom and the idea that it is more important to practice it than to enshrine it.

CONTENTS

WHY CONSIDER OPPOSING VIEWPOINTS?

"The only way in which a human being can make some approach to knowing the whole of a subject is by hearing what can be said about it by persons of every variety of opinion and studying all modes in which it can be looked at by every character of mind. No wise man ever acquired his wisdom in any mode but this."

John Stuart Mill

In our media-intensive culture it is not difficult to find differing opinions. Thousands of newspapers and magazines and dozens of radio and television talk shows resound with differing points of view. The difficulty lies in deciding which opinion to agree with and which "experts" seem the most credible. The more inundated we become with differing opinions and claims, the more essential it is to hone critical reading and thinking skills to evaluate these ideas. Opposing Viewpoints books address this problem directly by presenting stimulating debates that can be used to enhance and teach these skills. The varied opinions contained in each book examine many different aspects of a single issue. While examining these conveniently edited opposing views, readers can develop critical thinking skills such as the ability to compare and contrast authors' credibility, facts, argumentation styles, use of persuasive techniques, and other stylistic tools. In short, the Opposing Viewpoints Series is an ideal way to attain the higher-level thinking and reading skills so essential in a culture of diverse and contradictory opinions.

In addition to providing a tool for critical thinking, Opposing Viewpoints books challenge readers to question their own strongly held opinions and assumptions. Most people form their opinions on the basis of upbringing, peer pressure, and personal, cultural, or professional bias. By reading carefully balanced opposing views, readers must directly confront new ideas as well as the opinions of those with whom they disagree. This is not to simplistically argue that everyone who reads opposing views will—or should—change his or her opinion. Instead, the series enhances readers' understanding of their own views by encouraging confrontation with opposing ideas. Careful examination of others' views can lead to the readers' understanding of the logical inconsistencies in their own opinions, perspective on why they hold an opinion, and the consideration of the possibility that their opinion requires further evaluation.

EVALUATING OTHER OPINIONS

To ensure that this type of examination occurs, Opposing Viewpoints books present all types of opinions. Prominent spokespeople on different sides of each issue as well as well-known professionals from many disciplines challenge the reader. An additional goal of the series is to provide a forum for other, less known, or even unpopular viewpoints. The opinion of an ordinary person who has had to make the decision to cut off life support from a terminally ill relative, for example, may be just as valuable and provide just as much insight as a medical ethicist's professional opinion. The editors have two additional purposes in including these less known views. One, the editors encourage readers to respect others' opinions—even when not enhanced by professional credibility. It is only by reading or listening to and objectively evaluating others' ideas that one can determine whether they are worthy of consideration. Two, the inclusion of such viewpoints encourages the important critical thinking skill of objectively evaluating an author's credentials and bias. This evaluation will illuminate an author's reasons for taking a particular stance on an issue and will aid in readers' evaluation of the author's ideas.

As series editors of the Opposing Viewpoints Series, it is our hope that these books will give readers a deeper understanding of the issues debated and an appreciation of the complexity of even seemingly simple issues when good and honest people disagree. This awareness is particularly important in a democratic society such as ours in which people enter into public debate to determine the common good. Those with whom one disagrees should not be regarded as enemies but rather as people whose views deserve careful examination and may shed light on one's own.

Thomas Jefferson once said that "difference of opinion leads to inquiry, and inquiry to truth." Jefferson, a broadly educated man, argued that "if a nation expects to be ignorant and free . . . it expects what never was and never will be." As individuals and as a nation, it is imperative that we consider the opinions of others and examine them with skill and discernment. The Opposing Viewpoints Series is intended to help readers achieve this goal.

David L. Bender & Bruno Leone,
Series Editors

Greenhaven Press anthologies primarily consist of previously published material taken from a variety of sources, including periodicals, books, scholarly journals, newspapers, government documents, and position papers from private and public organizations. These original sources are often edited for length and to ensure their accessibility for a young adult audience. The anthology editors also change the original titles of these works in order to clearly present the main thesis of each viewpoint and to explicitly indicate the opinion presented in the viewpoint. These alterations are made in consideration of both the reading and comprehension levels of a young adult audience. Every effort is made to ensure that Greenhaven Press accurately reflects the original intent of the authors included in this anthology.

INTRODUCTION

"War in our time has been not merely a means of resolving inter-state disputes but also a vehicle through which the embittered, the dispossessed, the naked of the earth, the hungry masses yearning to breathe free, express their anger, jealousies, and pent-up urge to violence."
—John Keegan, A History of Warfare, 1993

During the twentieth century, the style of warfighting has changed many times. The first half of the century witnessed two world wars, multinational efforts that claimed millions of lives in the name of ending imperialism. These world wars were fought between grand alliances that committed conventional forces to the battlefield in hopes of wearing the other side down through attrition. The advent of the atom bomb and the coming of the nuclear age at the end of World War II made wars of attrition unnecessary. Nuclear weapons did not make conventional warfare obsolete, but they did ensure that conventional tactics could always be trumped by nuclear strike capabilities.

The two superpowers that possessed the greatest nuclear strike capacity—the United States and the Soviet Union—squared off against each other in a Cold War, during which neither was eager to confront the other on the battlefield. During this period, conventional wars continued to be fought in other nations. Some of these wars, such as the Arab-Israeli conflicts of the 1960s and 1970s, involved cross-border fighting. Others, such as the Korean War or the Vietnam War, were political struggles within a country's own borders. Unlike the world wars, these wars were not about global conquest and they did not jeopardize the safety of the world. A global war was not unthinkable, but its occurrence would likely include nuclear devastation, a possibility few nations were willing to court.

The world community—in the form of the United Nations (founded in 1945)—worked hard to resolve conflicts during the Cold War era. The United Nations was eager to play the role of arbiter to prevent isolated wars from spilling over their boundaries and draw in more countries, thus inviting superpower intervention. Unfortunately the effectiveness of the United Nations was often determined by the level of commitment of the United States, whose economic sanctions and military force are the backbone of the UN's bargaining power. The

United States could be slow to act, especially when its interests were not at stake. The tribal war in Rwanda in the mid-1990s is a case in point. After images of large-scale massacres of Rwandan civilians appeared on television, the United States reluctantly agreed to support the UN's efforts to prevent the slaughter from continuing. But by the time U.S. forces were committed to the small UN contingent, the major fighting was over and 500,000 to one million Rwandans had perished. One U.S. foreign policy analyst explained a possible reason for the delay in sending troops to halt the bloodbath:

> A genocidal campaign in Europe, in a country with modern cities like Sarajevo, seemed more disturbing than massacres of a far greater dimension on a continent where vast human suffering is a common occurrence.

The media has played a large part in bringing warfare to public attention. News coverage of the Vietnam War is thought to have had a great influence on the decision of the United States to withdraw from the conflict. On the other hand, media portrayals often prompt the world community to intervene in foreign wars. Columnist Jonathan Power even speculates that nations like the United States would get involved in more foreign conflicts if only the television broadcasters could find a way to make each war sensational and distinct. "American television itself can only manage one and a half foreign wars at a time," Power wryly asserts. "Public opinion is not engaged in Tadjikistan, Liberia or Rwanda, etc., because ever more heart-rending, anger-making pictures, night after night, are not there to wind it up."

After the collapse of the Soviet Union in 1991, new forms of warfare garnered media attention. In former Soviet states and Soviet-controlled satellites, crumbling communist governments opened the door to conflicts between different ethnic groups that had lived side by side for decades. With the fear of Soviet military reprisal lifted, ethnic groups in the former Yugoslavia fought to establish independent nations that were derived by ethnic and not national identity. In the Soviet Union itself the ethnic enclave of Chechnya tried to secede from Russia in the1990s. Ethnic warfare was not new to the world, but the number of nations wracked by ethnic strife did multiply in the post-Cold War period. "Ethnic cleansing" remains a media buzzword in the closing years of the twentieth century.

Faced with the rising number of ethnic conflicts the United Nations has had to adjust its role from peacemaker to peacekeeper. Caught between recognizing the validity of an ethnic group's fight for independence and the sovereign right of a country to resist the secession of its ethnic provinces, the UN has most often chosen to separate the warring factions with peacekeeping troops until some diplomatic resolution can be achieved. Unfortunately, these civil wars have placed UN soldiers in harm's way, making them targets for attack by the ethnic groups who are concerned only with separation, not arbitration. Media coverage of UN casualties can also lead to the weakening of a united peacekeeping effort. For example, footage of dead American soldiers being dragged through the streets of Mogadishu, Somalia, by an ethnic faction prompted the withdrawal of United States' troops from the UN peacekeeping mission in that nation during the early 1990s.

The major concern of the United Nations in dealing with these ethnic wars seems to be how to keep them from generating widespread conflict outside of their regional boundaries. The coming of another world war is still thought by many to be a real threat. In 1992, state department official George Kenney predicted that the conflict between ethnic Bosnians, Croats, and Serbs in the former Yugoslavia would inflame ethnic tensions in the Serbian province of Kosovo and cause the whole region to plunge Europe into another world war within six months. Kenney's prediction of global warfare has not materialized, but Kosovo did erupt in ethnic violence in 1998, and tensions there between Serbs and ethnic Albanians are only being held in check by the threat of NATO air strikes against the dominating Serbian forces. Behind all the talk of world war still lies the fear of nuclear devastation. With more nations gaining nuclear capabilities and a growing concern that Russian warheads may end up in the hands of foreign governments, the world retains part of its Cold War tension.

The issue of intervention as a means of maintaining peace is central to *War: Opposing Viewpoints*. Chapters entitled What Causes War? Should the International Community Intervene in the World's Conflicts? What Role Should the U.S. Play in Maintaining Peace? and How Can War Be Prevented? offer insight into the changing shape of twentieth-century warfare and the policies that are proffered to contend with and prevent it.

CHAPTER 1

|WHAT CAUSES WAR?

CHAPTER PREFACE

According to a 1998 study released by two Canadian psychologists who analyzed population patterns, the European conquest of the Americas, the Nazi aggression in World War II, the Iraqi invasion of Kuwait, and the ethnic wars in Africa and the former Yugoslavia may have begun in part because of an unusual demographic feature common to all. Christian G. Mesquida and Neil I. Wiener found a correlation between societies with a high percentage of young, unmarried, violence-prone men and the occurrence of wars. The psychologists contend that societies in which young males comprise 35 percent to 55 percent of the population are more likely to begin a war than societies which have a lower percentage of young men.

Mesquida and Wiener contend that a surplus of young males creates a shortage of land, food, and marriageable women. Although the men may not realize their true motivation for going to war, and may, in fact, claim they are fighting for political reasons, the psychologists assert that in evolutionary terms, many wars are "a form of intrasexual male competition among groups, occasionally to obtain mates but more often to acquire the resources necessary to attract and retain mates."

The authors maintain that their theory applies only to offensive, not defensive, wars. But, the authors argue, their study shows that a high number of young men is "a necessary condition for the emergence of violent conflicts." Furthermore, Mesquida and Wiener claim that their analysis can be used to identify potentially violent areas. For example, they assert, China may be facing a war in the near future as the number of men is expected to outnumber women by one million soon after the turn of the twenty-first century.

Population imbalances may be just one reason why wars are started. Other causes include politics, scarce resources, economics, religion, or a combination of these and other factors. The authors in the following chapter debate some of the reasons that motivate people and countries to war against their neighbors.

| "Some people do form tribes, and tribes do war, do seek war, choose war, do—dare I say it?—want war."

A Desire to Kill Causes War

Matthew Parris

Matthew Parris argues in the following viewpoint that some countries wage war sheerly because their inhabitants want to kill each other. Their desire to kill their enemies does not stem from insecurities, prejudice, or oppression, he contends, nor will their motivation to wage war disappear when their countries are at peace or if they have able leaders. Parris maintains that some people will fight simply because of blood lust. Parris is a writer for the London *Times*.

As you read, consider the following questions:

1. What was the author led to believe by his liberal, Christian education?
2. What is the doctrine of "false consciousness," according to Parris?
3. In the author's opinion, why do some liberals insist that a people's desire to wage war is not a real choice but a "pseudo-choice"?

Reprinted from Matthew Parris, "The Possible Explanation, Which We're Brought Up to Disbelieve, of Why People Kill Each Other," *The Spectator*, September 21, 1996, by permission; ©1996, The Spectator.

An unmentionable thought has long troubled me. With elections in the former Yugoslavia over, it is time to mention it. Perhaps the people in the Balkans really do want to kill each other.

Perhaps it isn't just fear which has made them nasty, and insecurity which exacerbates their nationalisms. Perhaps when their stomachs are full, their factories working, their fields tilled and order has returned to their lives they will not abandon but return, reinvigorated, to the old hatreds which wrecked their farms, emptied their stomachs and tore apart their world. Perhaps it's what they desire.

ETHNIC HATREDS ARE POTENT

Perhaps—heaven forbid—ethnic hatreds run on a fuel more potent than misunderstanding. Perhaps the Israelis would persecute the Arabs even if the Arabs stopped persecuting them; perhaps no ceasefire in the Middle East will end the Arab vendetta against the Israelis. Perhaps racism arises from more than ignorance.

Maybe education will not cure the sectarian divide in Ireland. Maybe Hutus and Tutsis in Rwanda and Burundi rape and pillage out of choice. Maybe tribes murder each other because they want to.

A LIBERAL, CHRISTIAN EDUCATION

Like many of my generation, I was given a liberal, Christian education. Not only at school but by precept and explanation at home I was taught that peace, love and mutual respect are the desired states of all sane men and women. The savageries in other lands about which we read in newspapers arose from ignorance, from fear and from hunger.

It followed that if poverty were eliminated and security established, if men and women had jobs to go to, crops in their fields, chickens in their pots and good books to read, and if people lost the fear of attack by others, they too would turn into liberal Christians like me. We would all support the United Nations. With education, everyone in the world would grow more and more like my family.

The Christian optimism of the third quarter of our century has translated itself into the liberal consensus of the fourth with little substantial change. People no longer so readily claim to be Christians, liberals or internationalists—we talk now of socialism, community values, 'democratic' values, 'combating ignorance' and 'the world order'—but the underlying assumptions are all still there: comfortable, untroubled, astonishingly unquestioned.

They should be questioned. We might question first the trusty shield for which every liberal reaches when the rocks begin to fly: the doctrine of 'false consciousness'. Karl Marx borrowed it from Christianity. Liberalism has taken it over from Marx.

It was Marx who coined the term 'false consciousness'; Christ said: 'They know not what they do'; your 1990s liberal falls back on key words like 'ignorance', 'illiteracy', 'fear', 'prejudice' or (recently) 'self-oppression'. But such formulations are linked by a single strand of reasoning. Confronted by another's apparently free choice to do something hateful, our belief in choice collides head-on with our belief in civilisation. To our embarrassment others have *chosen* to be uncivilised.

PSEUDO-CHOICE

Unwilling to abandon our commitment to democracy, we are obliged to insist that any settled decision to do something horrid could not have been a 'real' choice. It is therefore reclassified as a pseudo-choice. Jesus claimed that if people had not seen God, their decisions would be unknowing—not in the full sense decisions. Marx claimed that the proletariat had been subliminally cowed by the class structure into acting against their own class interest. Modern liberals claim it is fear and insecurity, hunger and ignorance, sexual repression, childhood abuse . . . anything, anything but that dreadful, nagging possibility, that thought we cannot quite banish, that individuals might as a matter of considered, unfettered choice, decide to behave like idiots.

A PERVERSE DESIRE TO DESTROY

World War I was hard to construe as in any way "rational," especially to that generation of European intellectuals, including Sigmund Freud, who survived to ponder the unprecedented harvest of dead bodies. History textbooks tell us that the "Great War" grew out of the conflict between "competing imperialist states," but this . . . interpretation has little to do with the actual series of accidents, blunders, and miscommunications that impelled the nations of Europe to war in the summer of 1914. At first swept up in the excitement of the war, unable for weeks to work or think of anything else, Freud was eventually led to conclude that there is some dark flaw in the human psyche, a perverse desire to destroy, countering . . . the will to live.

Barbara Ehrenreich, *Blood Rites: Origins and History of the Passions of War*, 1997.

The indoctrination begins early. 'No, Crispin,' one hears the middle-class mother in Sainsbury's reprove her child, 'you *don't* hate Rachel. You only think you do. But she's your little sister and you don't want to stick a green pepper in her mouth. You're just tired.'

'No, Mr Budgen,' one may hear Malcolm Rifkind reprove, kindly, the Member of Parliament for Wolverhampton SW, 'the Serbs, the Croats and the Bosnian Muslims don't all want to kill each other. They only think they do. It's just because they're frightened and insecure. Give them peace, security and elections, and they will choose harmony.'

Well, they haven't. But the liberal conscience has a fall-back position and you will hear it from Western leaders in the run-up to the decision (around Christmas 1995) not to withdraw our forces from the Balkans, contrary to the undertakings given. It isn't (we shall be assured) that peace cannot civilise the Balkans, it's just that they haven't had *enough* peace. We must give them a bit more. That should do the trick.

OTHER EXCUSES

Well, it won't. But even then there will be a fall-back position. This will be that the (only apparently) belligerent factions are 'badly led'. It's all [Bosnian Serb leader Radovan] Karadzic's fault.

One constantly hears this excuse for the bloody shambles into which Africa is turning: 'Such lovely people; badly led.' I've used it myself because I do love Africa and I cannot face what I ought to face: her peoples are bloodthirsty, tribalistic and count life cheap.

Then there's another excuse, another evasion: the cult of the Victim. To any conflict, one side must be an unwilling party, the other an unprovoked aggressor. By demonising one of the players we exonerate the others and are able to slot the drama comfortably into the category of 'moral tale', leaving us with somebody to support. There has been an attempt to do this with the Balkan story.

MEMORIES OF THE PAST

Finally—and to this, too, the former Yugoslavia has lent itself— the liberal conscience is forced back upon its last excuse: history. 'The bitterness of the past', we say, 'casts shadows forward', often blaming ourselves in part for that past. And this is the greatest liberal evasion of all, the illusion of a fundamentally blameless present which is somehow polluted by memory, by experience and by the sins of the dead; a future poisoned not by us and our friends, but by our grandfathers. History, not themselves, has foisted upon the Balkan peoples the future which they only seem to be choosing, but cannot choose.

And of course the past does have potency—who can deny it? But were the tribes who began the wars different animals from those who now continue them? Let us face the truth that some people do form tribes, and tribes do war, do seek war, choose war, do—dare I say it?—want war. When we have accepted that, we in Britain can make our own choice more honestly: what part do we wish our own sons and daughters to play in these wars?

| "People in former Yugoslavia did not kill each other because their moral condition falls lamentably short. . . . The war happened because of the particular aims of particular politicians."

GOVERNMENT POLICIES CAUSE WAR

Melanie McDonagh

In the following viewpoint, Melanie McDonagh refutes Matthew Parris's assertions that some people fight wars because they have a bloodthirsty desire to kill their enemies. For example, she argues, the war in former Yugoslavia occurred because of the actions and policies of its leaders. Furthermore, she contends, those who support the view that people war simply because they want to kill often base their opinions on ethnic prejudice. McDonagh is a reporter and columnist for the London *Evening Standard*.

As you read, consider the following questions:

1. Who were the victims during the war in Bosnia, according to McDonagh?
2. According to the author, what did most British policymakers believe about the war in Bosnia?
3. How did the arms embargo cost lives in the Bosnian war, in the author's opinion?

An unmentionable thought is troubling me, one that I have hardly dared articulate for several months. It is that the charming, influential and respected Matthew Parris is not the witty, refreshing, independent voice that I had supposed him to be. Rather he is in important respects a voice of the Establishment—his strictures about the British press, for instance, are not those of a hack among other hacks—and, more importantly, a columnist who sometimes articulates the Establishment's prejudices.

Don't misunderstand. In general, I am a great believer in not weighing down the fine impressionistic sweep of a column with fact. There are, however, occasions when an imperfect understanding can have horrible consequences and should, accordingly, not be flaunted. The war in former Yugoslavia is one such instance. Mr Parris gave a fine example of just such imperfect understanding in *The Spectator*.

'An unmentionable thought has long troubled me,' he writes. 'With elections in the former Yugoslavia over, it is time to mention it. Perhaps the people in the Balkans really do want to kill each other. Perhaps it isn't just fear which has made them nasty, and insecurity which exacerbates their nationalisms. Perhaps when . . . order has returned to their lives they will not abandon, but return, reinvigorated, to the old hatreds which . . . tore apart their world. Perhaps it's what they desire.'

UNTRUE THOUGHTS

The trouble is, opinion journalists are sometimes so captivated by having unmentionable thoughts, they forget to ask the more fundamental question: are they true? And in the case of Mr Parris's unmentionable thought, it is not true. People in former Yugoslavia did not kill each other because their moral condition falls lamentably short of that of Mr Parris. The war happened because of the particular aims of particular politicians, notably the policies of Serbian hegemony adopted by Slobodan Milosevic, backed by the Yugoslav Federal army. The cynical, immoral opportunism of the Zagreb government, once the dismemberment of Bosnia had taken place, worsened the problem.

VICTIMS AND AGGRESSORS

In Britain, I find, people instinctively make for the middle of the road; taking sides, even the right side against the wrong, is seen as simplistic, and therefore an error of taste. Mr Parris accordingly warns us against 'the cult of the Victim. To any conflict, one side must be an unwilling party, the other an unprovoked aggressor. By demonising one of the players we exonerate the others.'

Well, yes. There was a victim and an aggressor in this war. Some 70 per cent of Bosnia at one time was conquered by Bosnian Serb forces and all but a small number of non-Serbs were cleansed from that territory. The majority of these people were Muslims, mostly of an easy-going kind. They did not prepare for the war, they did not want the war; the war came to them when their neighbours, with weapons provided by the Federal army, directed by paramilitaries and mobilised by state-run media, arrived at their homes in force—they killed many of them, others were taken to concentration camps or prison, or simply brought to the front line and pushed over to the other side. Prijedor, Foca, Bijeljina, Brcko and Doboj are now almost wholly Serb precisely because of the phenomenon of unprovoked aggression in 1992. There was no comparable attempt to exterminate the Serbian population in Bosnian government territory during the war.

SALOON-BAR PREJUDICES

The other drawback to Mr Parris's unmentionable thought is not just that it is grotesquely wrong; it is that it has been mentioned in every quarter I can think of. Very far from saying the unsayable, Mr Parris is articulating saloon-bar prejudices which were held by most British policymakers. A senior British minister told a friend of mine in the Commons, at the very height of the conflict, that 'you have to understand that these people are just barbarous and primitive'. Indeed, if I have some sympathy with Mr Parris, it is that a sense of duty caused him to attend many if not all of the Commons debates on the subject of for-

---

POLITICAL CHOICES

Those who rejected the ethnic hatreds explanation for the war in former Yugoslavia emphasised the political causes of the war. They tended to characterise the conflict in Bosnia as a war of aggression waged by Serbia. Thus David Rieff rejected the "ancient ethnic hatreds" thesis and argued that it was the choice of the Serbian leader, Slobodan Milosevic, to invoke Serbian nationalism to further his political ambition of creating a "Greater Serbia": "There was nothing inevitable about the war there—it was the result of political choices, not national character or ancient historical bloodfeuds."

London International Research Exchange, *Journalists at War*, no date.

---

mer Yugoslavia. The ignorance and neo-colonialist prejudice displayed by most Members of Parliament were truly alarming.

The governmental and British army contempt for all the parties in Bosnia has rubbed off on the BBC: its correspondent in the region, Bob Simpson, remarked, in the context of the 1996 elections, that 'these people have been at each other's throats until a year ago—at least now they're going to the ballot box and not shooting each other', which is, in its way, a fine example of the misleading prejudice that one lot of primitive idiots is as bad as the next.

I agree that facts have less charm than the fine sweep of prejudice expressed in the 'ancient ethnic hatreds' idea. But the political background to the war has hardly been the preserve of a few obscure specialists. There have been some brilliant books published, notably Noel Malcolm's short history of Bosnia, and Alan Little and Laura Silber's account of the fall of Yugoslavia. As for those pundits who have set their faces on principle against the acquisition of information, they could at least have read *The Spectator*'s own admirable editorials on the war, which would have provided them with solid prejudices for next to no effort.

In a sense, it wouldn't have mattered that British politicians and military and journalists did not even try to understand the nature of the war, if Britain had not decisively intervened in the conflict. But the arms embargo was a really mortal consequence of the sort of attitude which Mr Parris articulates, that there was no real difference between the war aims of the parties in the conflict. Applied to all the armies alike, it served to consolidate the overwhelming superiority of the Serbs, who had the weaponry of the Federal army, and the overwhelming vulnerability of the Bosnian army, who started the war with hardly any weapons at all. Here, if nowhere else, careless thought cost lives.

I am sorry to take issue with Mr Parris in this fashion, but the consequences of the kind of beastly, lazy prejudice he articulates have been too painful and too bloody to allow me to take what he says in the normal spirit of iconoclastic journalism. Bosnia has been partitioned and an ethnic statelet has been established over the graves of the men of Prijedor and Srebrenica, in part because people like Matthew Parris went around saying the unsayable. The next time he has an unmentionable thought, perhaps he had better keep it to himself.

| "The next war in the Near East [will] not be about politics, but over water."

A SCARCITY OF FRESH WATER MAY LEAD TO WAR

Al J. Venter

The Middle East and North Africa have very limited supplies of fresh water. The rivers and aquifers supplying fresh water to the region are shared by countries that are not always at peace. In the following viewpoint, Al J. Venter asserts that peace and security in the region are dependent on the availability of adequate water supplies to all the affected countries. A decision or action by one country that affects the water supply of another country could lead to an international war, he maintains, as the affected country fights to secure its water rights. Venter is the Middle East correspondent for the London-based Jane's *International Defense Review* and a special correspondent for Jane's *Intelligence Review*. Jane's Information Group is considered the world's leading publisher of information on global defense, aerospace, and transportation.

As you read, consider the following questions:

1. Why does the United States not take the threat of war over water in the Middle East seriously, according to Boutros Boutros-Ghali, as cited by Venter?
2. What percentage of the world's fresh water supplies the needs of the Middle East and North Africa, according to the author?
3. Why have critics warned that the entire water supply of Gaza is at risk, according to the author?

Excerpted from Al J. Venter, "The Oldest Threat: Water in the Middle East," *Middle East Policy*, June 1998, by permission of *Middle East Policy*. Endnotes in the original have been omitted in this reprint.

F ormer U.N. Secretary General Boutros Boutros-Ghali, while
still a deputy minister in Cairo in 1985, said that the next war
in the Near East would not be about politics, but over water. Talking to Joyce Shira Starr, a senior associate at the Center for Strategic and International Studies in the American capital, he went on:
"Washington does not take this threat very seriously because everything in the U.S. relates to oil." Curiously, elsewhere in the region, it is maintained that he who controls Near East water resources dominates a large chunk of the world's oil supplies.

DISPUTES OVER WATER

Israeli Brigadier-General Zivka Kan-Tor takes a similar view. He
was posted as Military Attaché to the Southern African region
because of a reputation for his incisive analysis of complex
strategic issues. "Water," he told me during a visit to his extremely well-guarded Pretoria legation, "has had everything to
do with the conflicts of the recent past. The Six-Day War was
triggered by Egypt blockading the Gulf of Eilat (Aqaba) at Tiran.
Similarly, it was Israeli forces straddling Suez that caused Yom
Kippur; *more* water," he said.

So, too, was Syria drawn into the conflict because Israel sat
astride Golan and the Mount Hermon watershed. "And if you
look at what is happening along almost the entire length of the
Nile today, most disputes involving Ethiopia, the Sudan and
Egypt, again, center on water." He did make the point that each
time somebody talked policy in Israel these days, security issues
were invariably equated to the availability of adequate supplies
of water.

General Kan-Tor mentioned one of the last statements made
by [Israeli prime minister Yitzhak] Rabin before he was assassi-
nated [in 1995]. Speaking on the question of Golan and the
possibility of Syrian domination of the heights above Lake
Kineret (Sea of Galilee), the prime minister declared that he
couldn't see that happening if agreements about water usage
were not coupled to iron-clad guarantees. Preferably they should
be underwritten by a major power, he said. "The uninterrupted
supply of water to the nation is more important than peace," he
concluded; the comment, made off the cuff, is profound. It un-
derscores Israel's *sine qua non* with regard to any future peace settlement with Syria or, for that matter, anyone else in the region.

Of all the issues facing millions living in the Near East, the
most immediate and least understood, is that of the availability
of potable water. The entire region is facing a critical shortage
because there is simply not enough of it. For instance, there are

those who say that if Jordan cannot reach a long-term accord with Israel on the supply of water, Amman could be "dry" in a generation. Dr. John Kolars, the preeminent authority on the subject is not so sure.

Elsewhere, claims and counterclaims have inflamed already emotional sentiments. The problem is pertinent in the most arid of the world's regions. Israel is involved in a succession of water disputes with Syria, Lebanon and Jordan, as well as with the Palestinian Authority within its own borders. Syria and Iraq, together, are locked in bitter acrimony with Turkey over the flow of the Euphrates. As populations increase at a frightening pace, the equation becomes even more intractable, especially since most of those involved are, if not wary of one another, then downright suspicious.

In his book on the Syrian capital, *Mirror to Damascus*, which was published in 1967, Colin Thubron wrote elegantly about what was then still one of the beautiful rivers of the region, the Barada. "Cool river" he called it. He talked about its sweet waters that had quenched thirst since time began.

THE SITUATION CAN ONLY GET WORSE

No more. When I visited Syria in 1997, the Barada was a river in name only. Its flow had slowed measurably. In central Damascus it was so polluted it stank. Yet, there was a time when the Barada supported hundreds of generations of people in the world's oldest continuously inhabited city. Now Damascenes are dependent on the run-off from the nearby mountains. Aleppo, Syria's second city gets by on water piped from the Euphrates, a month-long camel ride away. Strategists have suggested that the Israelis could destroy both links in a single air strike.

Other water resources in the region are prone to disputes: Lebanon's Litani and the Orontes; the Yarmuk, which flows southwards out of Syria and yields a healthy 570 million cubic/meters (mcm) a year, though it is seasonal; the Jordan, as well as a variety of subterranean water sources or aquifers which are not only over-utilized, but badly contaminated. In some areas, salinity is many times the accepted level.

And since the Israelis and Palestinians are deadlocked over these and other issues, this scenario, mostly bitter and often contentious, can only get worse. . . .

WATER IN THE MIDDLE EAST

To understand the full implications of some of the problems facing the Near East, it is essential to view matters in a global context. While water is the world's most abundant resource, most of it is in the oceans (70 percent of the earth's surface is covered with water and 97 percent of that is seawater). Of the remaining freshwater (3 percent of the globe's total liquid resources) roughly nine-tenths is locked in ice caps, glaciers, the atmosphere, soil or deep aquifers. Consequently about 13 percent of what is left (or less than one half of one percent) is drinkable. And barely a single percentage point of all that is in the Middle East and North Africa (including the Nile).

An Important Variable

The insufficiency of fresh water has in the past led to violent conflict, and is currently the source of international tensions, but one should not simply assume that population growth will inevitably lead to war over water. Technology, pricing, conservation, trade, and industrial and agricultural policy changes may mitigate water scarcity and alter the prescription for conflict. Research on environmental security issues generally accepts the multiple causes of conflict, but fresh water is undeniably an important variable. Given assumed population growth, changes in climatic conditions, and the imbalance of water resource supply and demand, it will continue as a source of tensions; it could become the determinant variable in future international conflict.

Kent Hughes Butts, *Parameters*, Spring 1997.

In the entire region, the most severely affected area is Gaza. Increasingly, critics have warned that Gaza's entire water supply in an area of 200 square miles fringing the Mediterranean is at serious risk. Some is unacceptable because of its salinity. Also, it has been polluted by effluent and human waste seepage, largely because of inadequate sanitation. There is also the problem of seawater entering the aquifer because of over-utilization. Affected are almost a million people, many of them refugees. A large proportion are living more than 100,000 to the square mile in single-story housing.

The World Bank, in a report published in March 1996, stated that the situation in Gaza "is more acute than anywhere else in the world." Gaza residents, according to John Hayward, its director of agriculture and water-resources management, "have access to 15 gallons of water per person per day, a very different situation from the West Bank where the figure is 40 gallons pppd." The situation had become untenable, he stated.

Earlier, issues had been exacerbated by a Knesset economics

committee statement that "Gaza must solve its shortages with water from the Nile, not from Israel." In Cairo some observers regarded that comment as war talk.

Crucially, population growth and associated water use have reduced the limited per-capita water supply in Gaza to a third of its 1960s level. More significant, with the population in the region growing at more than 4 percent a year, these resources are expected to halve over the next 30 years.

Other parts of the Near East are similarly affected. Jordan and Yemen have been withdrawing 25 to 30 percent more from aquifers than is being replenished. "They are destroying their capital by mining groundwater," the World Bank states. In Gaza this resource is being mined even faster. . . .

As Brigadier-General Kan-Tor has said, one needs to listen very carefully to statements made by Israeli leaders these days, especially those that emanate from Prime Minister Benjamin Netanyahu. Water in the Holy Land has suddenly become a rather emotional issue.

Israel derives 80 percent of its 600 mcm of water from three aquifers that originate in what it calls Judea and Samaria, the West Bank. The Western aquifer (which flows to the coast) and provides Tel Aviv with much of its needs, produces more than half. The northern aquifer extends from Jenin to the Mt. Gilboa area and gives the Jezreel Valley and Beit Shean what it needs with a yield of 140 mcm a year. The eastern aquifer has the potential to supply 170 mcm, or about 50 percent more than its current output.

PALESTINIANS AND WATER

With the Palestinian Authority (PA) dominating large areas that were formerly controlled by Israel, there are fears that there will now be a spate of uncontrolled well-drilling, which could eventually disrupt or contaminate the flow. Former Labor agriculture minister Yaacov Tzur said in a public statement that "if the Palestinians (continue to do this) they will take away our water. It's as simple as that." Tzur's statement was made for the gallery. Anyone who understands the geological structure of the region is aware that it is very hard to drill a karasic limestone foundation. The filters clog very readily. The underground water will flow as it always has.

For their part, the Palestinians argue that they should be able to drill as and where they please. After all, it is their land. And in any event, water and land are inseparable, they maintain. Critics of this contention have pointed out that both international law and Arab customary law acknowledge traditional usage as *primer inter pares* [first among equals]. Palestinian claims to the exclusive use of those aquifers has no basis in law. Tzur's comment was prompted by Palestinian unwillingness to cooperate on the matter. Left long enough, the Israelis reckon, two of the three aquifers will be overextended and the salinity level will be irrevocably increased if drastic steps are not taken immediately.

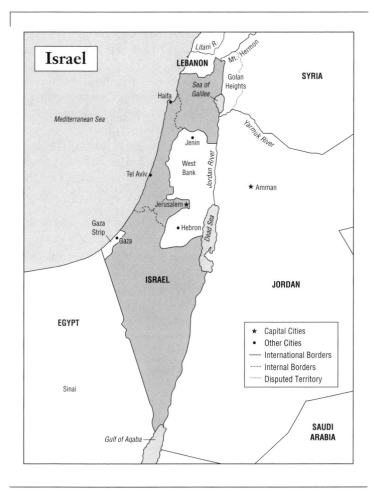

In contrast, the Palestinians maintain that their people use only a fraction of the water that the Jewish community has at its disposal. They back their argument with figures: the average family in Haifa or Tel Aviv uses 100 cubic meters of household water per family compared to the Palestinian's 40 cm (and California's 200).

In his statement, Tzur asserted that Israel would maintain water supervision over areas from which the Israeli Defense Force (IDF) withdraws, largely to ensure that Palestinians do not tap groundwater without approval. Jerusalem also demands the right to certify the quality of the water and the disposal of sewage in the autonomous region. Both points have been rejected by the PA. What is of consequence is that pollution is at least as serious a problem for the underground water as sharing. The Palestinians could unwittingly pollute Israel's drinking water. In that limestone foundation it would be impossible to clean up.

Even more radical was Tzur's (and his successor's) demand that Israel (and not the PA) supply water directly to Jewish settlements and that major Jewish communities in Palestinian areas have separate lines to Mekorot (the Israeli water authority). Some of Yaser Arafat's followers say that this is absurd—and a waste of money. It is not Palestinian security that is threatened, the Israelis counter. And so the argument goes on. There was much concern, especially in Washington, that the gap between the two positions over such a sensitive matter led to a breakdown on the first day of water negotiations. Since then the situation has eased, but some of the problems are unresolved. . . .

THE NILE

And then there is the Nile, which Ronald Bleier examined in great detail in an issue of *Middle East Policy*. He left one issue unaddressed. Why is Egypt so determined to go ahead with its Sinai water projects in the face of good advice to the contrary? [Egyptian president Hosni] Mubarak is also flaunting Egyptian public opinion. This can be dangerous considering Egypt's undercurrent of domestic tensions. It is necessary, too, to question the logic of proceeding with a project that might be of some economic advantage to Israel. The pipeline that Egypt has built stretches all the way to an area adjacent to Gaza's El Arish. Now there is talk of pushing it through still further.

This is an unusual development. Israel for many years was the implacable enemy of all Egyptians. And while there is an uneasy peace between the two countries now, even the Americans have to concede that the measure of mistrust between Jerusalem and Cairo is palpable. . . .

Critics argue [that] if diverted Nile waters result in a large proportion of Israel's Palestinian community becoming dependent on Egyptian goodwill (Gaza, especially, where the situation is already critical), President Mubarak might end up with powerful political leverage. Perhaps that is exactly what he is aiming for. Even his enemies acknowledge that Mubarak is a shrewd and, when he has to be, a ruthless visionary. He would then, as an Israeli strategist at Tel Aviv's Moshe Dayan Institute phrased it, "have pushed us into a corner from which we might not be able to extricate ourselves because the taps would be on the other side of the Suez Canal." Should that happen, my source indicated, there would almost certainly be another war.

"Prohibitions against worshipping
other gods have led to intolerance,
hatred, and even destruction of those
who have other religious beliefs."

RELIGIOUS INTOLERANCE CAN LEAD TO WAR

Roger Brooks

Many of the world's wars are fought by people of different faiths. In the following viewpoint, Roger Brooks asserts that religious intolerance has led religious leaders and their followers to misunderstand and stereotype people of other faiths. Such divisions can lead to hatred and violence or warfare between different religious groups, he maintains. Roger Brooks is the Elie Wiesel Professor of Judaic Studies at Connecticut College in New London.

As you read, consider the following questions:
1. How does the admonition to worship no other god lead to religious intolerance, according to Brooks?
2. Why does Brooks prefer the term "Jew-hatred" to anti-Semitism?
3. What are the three bases for Jew-hatred in the twentieth century, in the author's opinion?

Abridged from Roger Brooks, "Why Do We Hate Each Other?" USA Today magazine, March 1994. Reprinted by permission of the Society for the Advancement of Education, ©1994.

R eligious hatred and violence run rampant throughout the entire civilized world. Ireland remains torn by fighting between Protestants and Catholics. In Bosnia, Muslims are undergoing "ethnic cleansing"—an antiseptic euphemism for mass murder! India's Sikhs and Hindus routinely clash, burning houses of worship and killing one another. Israelis and Palestinians die in strife between religious visions of the Holy Land. The list of religiously inspired conflicts goes on and on.

RELIGION AS A POSITIVE FORCE

How strangely ironic it is for violence to be sanctioned in the name of religion! Throughout history, religions more often have been a positive force in promoting human culture. Think of the great advances of ethical monotheism, of the Ten Commandments and Jewish ethics and law. Consider also the stunning intellectual achievements of 12th- and 13th-century Islamic philosophers, who singlehandedly preserved and transmitted the classics of Greek thought, systematized mathematics (al-gebra is an Arabic word), and took poetic analysis to new heights. Christian theology, both on its own and in response to these Muslim intellectual initiatives, produced the very staples of Western culture. Yet again, recall the uplifting and deeply spiritual literature of Hindu epics, Confucian philosophy, and the Hebrew Bible.

American culture has been much improved by its foundation in the Bible. On a social level, biblical tradition stands behind beliefs in blind justice ("You shall have but one law for rich and poor!"); in careful and truthful examination of witnesses in court ("Justice and only justice shall you pursue!"); of punishment that fits the crime ("If the criminal deserves punishment . . . he shall receive it in proportion to his crime!"). On an interpersonal level, the Bible provides the bases of our ethics ("Do not place a stumbling block before the blind!" or anyone else for that matter); laws protecting life ("You shall not murder!"); family stability ("You shall not commit adultery!"); and religious tolerance ("The stranger among you shall be as the homeborn . . . for you once were strangers in the land of Egypt: I the Lord am your God!"). On a personal level, biblical admonitions attempt to build character, true to people's selves, desiring nothing ("You shall not covet!"), and swearing only to the truth ("You shall not bear false witness!"). Indeed, the ethical legacy of the Bible—and of all religion—is uplifting, not full of hate.

Somehow, though, the world has turned against these uplifting religious messages. Prohibitions against worshipping other gods have led to intolerance, hatred, and even destruction of those who have other religious beliefs. Biblical war legends—in context clearly meant to "grandfather" the Land of Israel for the Jews—now are taken as justification for armed struggle. The Islamic *jihad* (holy war) is but one example. Messianic predictions from the Bible encouraged David Koresh and his Branch Davidian followers to amass a frightening arsenal of weapons, arms they all too clearly were willing to use to defend themselves against outsiders.

What lies at the root of this misuse of religion? There is a straightforward correlation between exclusivity and intolerance. When religions hold to an absolute claim on the truth, they turn inward, marking outsiders as "The Other." If I am really right and *you* disagree, then *you* must be wrong. Notice how this rhetoric places the issue in stark, black-and-white terms. The emphasis is not on "what you *believe* is wrong," which allows for interesting discussion, but on "*You* are wrong," which brands an individual and makes value judgments explicitly personal. By contrast, when religions take a more measured and pluralistic view, they tend to turn outward, welcoming the best of each culture and its special wisdom.

It is the recent worldwide trend toward fundamentalism and absolutism that has led religions to promote hatred, or at least to sanction it in the name of a higher authority. Nowhere is this better expressed than by Tom Lehrer, a professor turned satirical songwriter, in his tune "National Brotherhood Week": "Oh, the Protestants hate the Catholics,/and the Catholics hate the Protestants,/and the Hindus hate the Moslems,/but everybody hates the Jews. . . ."

JEW-HATRED

The song is right. Among the many ethnic and racist hatreds, anti-Semitism once again runs rampant in the world today. Listen to these charges leveled in recent years: Jewish doctors in Chicago inject black babies with the AIDS virus in order to do away with them; Jews want abortions kept legal because they control the medical profession and make their money by providing abortions; the Jews are plotting secretly to take over the entire world. All three of these—and worse, no doubt—have made the rounds, the first two in the tabloid press and the third in Japan, where *The Protocols of the Elders of Zion*, a Russian fabrication from the late 1800s, has made the bestseller list.

It is important to come right out and call this type of prejudice what it is: Jew-hatred. That name is as coarse and base as the idea is—like ethnic cleansing, "anti-Semitism" somehow is too polite and antiseptic. The world can categorize (and thus minimize) anti-Semitism, but the more direct and obviously prejudicial "Jew-hatred" may shock people into realization of what is really at stake.

Of course, Jews can be haters, too. For centuries, they have been victims of religious intolerance and thus hatred; no one should think that Jews are essentially exempt from these same tendencies. I teach a course on the Holocaust at Connecticut College. One of my students, as part of a class assignment, was supposed to interview a Holocaust survivor. The student had a difficult time contacting one, but finally a rabbi took her name and promised to have an acquaintance of his, a concentration camp survivor, call my pupil. When their phone conversation began, everything went well at first. The survivor asked my student why she wanted to conduct this interview ("It's a class assignment"), how she knew the rabbi ("He lives nearby"), and why she was interested in the Holocaust. My student answered, truthfully, that, as a Catholic, she decried the Church's inaction during the Nazi years. "You are a Catholic?," the survivor demanded, then launched into a tirade about how every Catholic and every Pole should be damned to hell, and hung up.

I tell this story not to invalidate the feelings of that woman who survived the death camps—I can not judge her experiences or feelings. I simply want to point out that, for whatever reason, it is not hard to find Jews who have become resentful, even hateful toward others. Religious intolerance and hatred is not a one-way street. That kind of traffic moves back and forth all too easily.

THREE BASES FOR HATRED

Yet, if the goal is to come to some understanding of religious prejudice and baseless hatred, people will do well to focus on Jew-hatred. Not only is it persistent and omnipresent, but also structurally broad and encompassing. Jew-hatred has three separate bases in the 20th century—religion, nationality, and race.

Religion. Christian Jew-hatred gripped the people of Europe and operated at a theoretical level, in the assertion that Jews had killed Jesus and should therefore be despised. At a more practical level, Christians hated Jews simply because they were different.

Nationality. The rise of nation-states across Europe placed the Jews in a precarious position. They were subject to ever-increasing pressure as a nation within the state or, more precisely, as a nation without a state.

Race. "Scientific" theories at the end of the 19th century created a racial hierarchy of humanity that placed Jews—together with all non-Europeans—at the bottom.

LIBERATING LAND FROM THE INFIDELS

As the Arabs see it, Allah placed the oil in their land to produce massive, all-empowering revenues to enable them to promote their religion. Since they regard the occupation of Muslim lands by infidels as blasphemous, they are obliged in theory to liberate them. . . .

Lately they have had initial unexpected success in Bosnia-Herzegovina. . . . What had been a one-third Muslim minority [has turned] into a Muslim state.

Alfred Sherman, *Spectator*, March 14, 1998.

Because of this broad foundation, careful study of Jew-hatred leads to understanding of all types of prejudice, even those with narrower causes. Anti-Semitism can serve as an example that will allow people to comprehend an entire century of hatred, and perhaps help them move beyond this hatred as a new millennium approaches.

Colleges and universities often are thought of as populated by young, open minds, eager to learn about others, yearning to explore strange new worlds intellectually. To be sure, this intellectual liberalism works against certain kinds of prejudices and hatred.

PROUD OF THEIR HATE

However, campuses also are places where hateful speech and action abound. Quite often, these young, open minds make use of new-found intellectual space to try on the ignorant insensitivities they have encountered throughout their lives. All too often, they wear this ignorance as a badge of pride. Here are two examples of this almost boastful prejudice:

• When I taught Judaic Studies at the University of Notre Dame, I was assigned to teach a seminar for 15 first-year students. I explained in the first class meeting that the topic of our study would be classical Jewish religious literature. I received little response for about 10 minutes. Finally, one of the students raised his hand and politely asked, "Are you a Jew?" After I told him I was, his next question almost floored me: "Well, then, where are your horns and tail?" At first, I thought this was his idea of a bad joke; but let me assure you, I was the first Jew he had met, and at some level he was unprepared for my unadorned appearance.

• Two years later, I was teaching the same course. In a rapid overview of Jewish history, from the Bible to modern times, I spent 10 minutes on 20th-century anti-Semitism and the Holocaust, ending by remarking, "Thank God the Nazis did not succeed in destroying all of European Jewry." Then one young man chimed in, "At least if they had, we wouldn't have to take this stupid class!" The bravado with which that line was delivered new has left me.

What is the first thought I had after these incidents? I left class thinking I should call the dean, who could remove the students and work with them on their attitudes. However, kicking the students out would have been a mistake. That would have left them smug in their ignorance and would have fed them intolerance.

Such students need a course in Judaica. It was fairly simple to explain the biblical mistranslation behind my student's centuries-old fallacy: "Moses came down with rays of light shining from his face" long ago had been mistranslated as ". . . with horns rising from his face." Yet, I did have to teach him that Jews have no horns, are not demonic, and are not in league with Satan. Although we usually think of such attitudes as no longer current, here they are before our eyes.

Small tokens of success in such endeavors can be found. One of those in that first seminar, on a student course evaluation, paid me what he thought was a huge compliment: "I came to Notre Dame, an all-Catholic school, and ended up learning from a Jew what true spirituality is!" His exposure to Judaic Studies in an academic setting may have inoculated him for life against the virus of Jew-hatred.

> "Debt [can] spawn the complete collapse of law and order, war between different ethnic or national groups, even genocide."

A Ruined Economy Can Lead to Civil War

Ken Coates

In the following viewpoint, Ken Coates argues that countries that are extremely impoverished and overwhelmed with national debt are at risk for war. Such economies are unstable, he contends, and their governments frequently disintegrate, resulting in social chaos and the breakdown of law and order. From there, Coates asserts, it is a short step to war, ethnic cleansing, and genocide. Coates is an English member of the European Parliament.

As you read, consider the following questions:

1. How does poverty aggravate the destruction of the environment, according to Coates?
2. What is "capability poverty," as defined by the author?
3. How should the world intervene when impoverished countries slide into wars or genocide, in the author's opinion?

Excerpted from Ken Coates, "Poverty and Peace," *Peace Review*, vol. 10, no. 1 (March 1998), p. 89. Reprinted by permission.

Only yesterday, it seems, the Berlin Wall was taken to pieces, and academic journals began to bubble with exciting chatter about the end of history. Some decommissioning of nuclear weapons followed, by agreement, but large arsenals remained to rust and rot, leeching poisons into the environment. In previous years, there had been extensive discussions about how we could use the peace dividend. But for all too many people, the peace dividend was drawn in the unemployment benefit offices, if indeed they were fortunate enough to live in countries that actually compensated people for the loss of their jobs.

The end of the Cold War has not put the armorers out of business, even if it has changed some of the flows within the world arms trade. That trade remains swollen, and no previous age has ever been so militarized. The Cold War's end has neither brought about a great renovation of the United Nations Organization nor promoted any wide-ranging new forms of international cooperation. Instead, within the global economy we have seen a continuation, and on occasion, an acceleration of harmful trends which were already perfectly clear when the arms race was in full flood and when the conflict between East and West seemed a fixture, permanent to the point of ritual. Internally, the U.N. remains torn, indebted, and crisis prone. Externally, the world it serves is no better off. . . .

THE EFFECTS OF POVERTY

Gro Harlem Brundtland, the Prime Minister of Norway, reported in *Our Common Future*, prepared for the World Commission on the Environment in 1987:

> There are more hungry people in the world today than ever before in human history, and their numbers are growing. In 1980 there were 340 million people in 87 developing countries not getting enough calories to prevent stunted growth and serious health risks. . . . The World Bank predicts that these numbers are likely to go on growing.

This poverty was aggravating the destruction of the natural environment. Often this destruction was driven by high levels of debt, so that the rain forests were uprooted, species were eliminated, irreplaceable resources destroyed, in order to raise the wherewithal, not even to pay off past borrowings, but to keep up interest payments. In Madagascar 93% of the original forest had gone by the time Ms. Brundtland reported. It was estimated that possibly 6,000 varieties of plants, each one unique, had been killed off. . . .

Russia Regresses

The Soviet Union at its peak of development registered very substantial advances in education and in health. The health gains were already in jeopardy in the 1980s, as was exposed in a series of dissident writings about alcoholism and increased morbidity. Since 1991 Russia's growth and human development have been arrested. Mass unemployment and poverty, rampant inequality of incomes, and severe alienation have all reacted to reduce life expectancy. In 1989 male life expectancy was 64 years, already lower than it had been earlier. But by 1995 it had fallen to 57.3. Female life expectancy was also falling, from 74 plus to 70. Infant mortality is now four times higher than that in the United States. Homicides, suicides, and accidental deaths are increasing. If matters so close to home are beyond the Russian government's influence, it is not surprising that global inequalities should prove beyond its reach. Far from helping overcome Third World poverty, Russia is already suffering widespread poverty and is itself moving towards Third World status. Other parts of the former communist world have suffered even more dire developments while the accumulation of debt and misery has not ceased throughout large areas of the underdeveloped world.

Indeed, debt burgeoned throughout the developing world between the oil price crisis and the beginning of the 1990s. Total developing country debts were $160 billion in 1975, $1,160 billion in 1992. Debt in Sub-Saharan Africa increased tenfold from 30 billion to 300 billion during the same period. In 1996, the United Nations Development Program (U.N.D.P.) published its Development Report, dedicated to showing that there is more to "development" than can be shown in the economic statistics. Even so, the statistics were no less ominous than before.

"If present trends continue, economic disparities between the industrial and developing nations will move from inequitable to inhuman," the report said. In purely economic terms, almost 70 countries could count the 1980s a "lost decade." For them, in 1990, average incomes were lower than they had been in 1980. Forty-three countries now had average incomes lower than they had been in 1970. Back in 1960, the richest 20% of the world's population were 30 times better off than the poorest 20%. Now, they were 61 times richer. All this could be graphically expressed in one simple finding: "The wealth of the world's 358 billionaires exceeds the combined annual incomes of countries which are home to nearly half the world's people."

Polarization in its more benign form could, perhaps, enrich the few without absolutely depressing the many. But in the years after 1989, this relatively benign process turned mean. In 21 countries, average incomes fell by one-fifth or more. Most of these countries were in the Commonwealth of Independent States or in Eastern Europe, which were witnessing the depravities of gangster capitalism alongside the benefits of the rhetoric of democracy.

Over three decades, the proportion of people enjoying per capita income growth of 5% a year or more increased more than twofold (12 to 27%). But the proportion of people experiencing negative growth multiplied itself by more than three (5 to 18%). There was also a threefold increase in the size of the gap in the per capita incomes of the industrial and developing worlds, each taken as a whole.

The dynamic forces behind this polarization are a few hundred giant companies, which mine or manufacture at least half the world's total output. Each of the traded raw materials that go into our food and other consumer goods are now marketed by a handful of transnational corporations. In every sector, three or four giant corporations now account for 80–90% of the world's commodities. In the most modern industries, concentration runs further, faster. Twenty-three electronics corporations account for 80% of world sales, and just five of them are responsible for half of all foreign sales.

"CAPABILITY POVERTY"

True, the U.N.D.P. shows that human development can be sustained even while the economy lags. It registers impressive advances in the transmission of new skills, and conversely shows that "capability poverty" is more prevalent than "income poverty" in developing countries. Poverty is normally conceived of as a lack of income. Taking an arbitrary figure, the U.N.D.P. gives us an example: "If one dollar a day is taken as the poverty line, thirty-three percent of the developing world's population, or 1.3 billion people, is poor." Almost half of these people live in South Asia, a quarter of them in Sub-Saharan Africa.

But "capability poverty" by contrast measures not what is in the pocket, but instead the average state of human endowment. The measure devised was constructed to look at health, reproduction, and education. It identifies precise measures. Not health in general, but the precise proportion of children under five who are underweight. Not simply the birth rate, but the proportion of births unattended by midwives or other qualified personnel. Not all educational attainments, but the precise numbers of family illiterates. An index compiled from these data directly reflects the improvement or deterioration of the social condition. Twenty-one per cent of the people in developing countries live below the income poverty line, but 37% of them are below the capability poverty thresholds. In other words, 900 million people in developing countries are income poor, but 1.6 billion are capability poor.

ECONOMIC DEVELOPMENT IS ESSENTIAL

The essential policies of [war] prevention—early warning, preventive diplomacy, preventive deployment and preventive disarmament—will succeed only if the root causes of conflict are addressed. . . .

These causes are often economic and social. Poverty, endemic underdevelopment and weak or non-existent institutions inhibit dialogue and invite the resort to violence. A long, quiet process of sustainable economic development, based on respect for human rights and legitimate government is essential to preventing conflict.

Kofi Annan, speech to the Foreign Affairs Committee of the Chinese People's Political Consultative Conference, April 2, 1998.

These figures could be susceptible to change, not only as a result of beneficial growth, if such a thing were to happen. A major change could come from statistical interpretation, since efforts are now being made to register and count the value of unpaid work, most of which is done by women. Two-thirds of women's work time goes unrecorded, and if guesstimates about this enter the statistics, then clearly outcomes change. To record the fact that Indian women work 69 hours a week on average, while in Moldova the tally runs at 74 hours a week is to recognize an injustice to women. The U.N.D.P. records that "In Japan women's work burden is about seven percent higher than men's, in Austria, eleven percent higher, and in Italy twenty-eight percent higher." Nonetheless, if the national per capita income is augmented by estimates such as this, nothing will have been done to diminish the real effect of income poverty.

At one level, the effects of poverty are measured in personal unhappiness: deprivation and malnutrition. Where there is runaway poverty, there may be famines, mass migration of populations, and rampant disease and mortality. But widespread debt also destroys local economies, shreds political authority, and feeds social chaos. In that way lies ruin. Michael Barratt Brown has examined three of the approaches to ruin, none of which, unfortunately, is likely to prove unique. They are the paths taken by Yugoslavia, Peru, and Rwanda-Burundi. In these cases, debt leaps over the impoverishment of peoples to spawn the complete collapse of law and order, war between different ethnic or national groups, even genocide.

YUGOSLAVIA

The disintegration of Yugoslavia is normally explained by the growth of tension between ethnic groups, resulting in runaway xenophobia and culminating in ethnic cleansing. At the end of the process, the war in Yugoslavia certainly produced more than enough atrocities, massacres, and brutal conflicts. But how was Yugoslavia torn apart? Rising debt had been a feature of the Yugoslav economy since the oil price hike, which both necessitated loans and ensured that the banks could make them with recycled oil moneys. By 1988, the debt burden amounted to one-third of the Yugoslav national product, and a quarter of annual exports were needed simply to service it.

Unemployment shot up to more than 50% of the urban population, but since most of the work done was directly for the export market, there was a famine in consumer goods at home. Inflation rocketed from 15% at the end of the 1970s to 1,300% at the end of the 1980s. A currency conversion was carried through in 1990 to meet this problem, with the result that most people lost their savings. Because of the large migration of Yugoslav workers over many years, part of the population had earned Deutschmarks or Lira, and these currencies became the staple upon which large parts of the population depended. Tensions between Yugoslavia's component nationalities rose as the Federal Government sought to persuade them all to make a contribution to the resolution of the debt problem. These tensions were fostered and encouraged by external powers seeking to improve their economic penetration of the region.

No one will seek to downplay the resultant horrors of the war in former Yugoslavia. But it is necessary to remember that the origins of this war did not lie in ethnic animosities, but in unbearable levels of debt. The animosities grew, for sure, to fill the space available, but it was debt that created that space.

PERU

Barratt Brown also tells the very different story of Peru, where debt has fostered the trade in coca. Peruvian debt piled up in the late 1960s and early 1970s, very much in connection with the militarization of government and society. Huge arms imports were necessary to enable military adventures against neighboring states, in order to divert popular attention from the lack of food, as well as the lack of human rights. By the 1980s, the servicing of the debt needed more than half the country's total export earnings. Unemployment rose, and inflation shot up to 2,772% in 1989. As real wages were cut in half, 100,000 Peruvians left the country.

These were the dramatic circumstances in which cocaine production grew and grew. More than half Latin America's coca comes from Peru, where the land area planted with this crop has increased tenfold during the last decade. Debt found its solution here, at a cost that must be paid elsewhere, in the destruction of normal standards in the inner cities and ghettos of countries very far away from the Andean highlands.

RWANDA

The third of Barratt Brown's examples is Rwanda. When the Belgians pulled out in 1962, a long descent into violence began. In Rwanda the Hutus overthrew the Tutsis, while in Burundi, a Tutsi army seized power. All efforts at reconciliation came to grief. Thousands died in 1972 and tens of thousands in 1988. Half a million is the lowest estimate of the latest slaughter, 1994. But these blood storms do not have their origins in ethnic conflict. The degradation and exhaustion of the soil has turned Rwanda into "a potential and quite often an actual wasteland." Panic expansion of export crops has sought to stave off the pressures of foreign creditors. As a result, in the 1980s, coffee prices collapsed. By 1990 Burundi had to devote more than 40% of its export earnings to debt servicing. In Rwanda, the tally ran at more than 20%. Excessive cash cropping results in soil degradation, and the weakening of the rural economy inevitably provokes migration. Basil Davidson points up the chain of disorder, from rural impoverishment to migration, and then, with easy access to automatic firearms, the slide into genocide:

> The reasons for the spread of automatic weapons simply follow: in such conditions good government loses heart and disappears. Even moderately bad government ceases to be achievable. The mindless coups d'etat multiply. The bandits take over.

Facing such situations the United Nations is the only international organization with the lingering credibility to intervene. But U.N. action has constantly been directed at the consequences of debt rather than its causes. Of course, when shooting wars break out in Somalia or Bosnia, or when human rights atrocities reach unimaginable levels, world public opinion looks for action. If such action were to be rationally based, then it would begin with the cancellation of the foreign debts of the poorest Third World countries. Some of these debts are owed directly to banks in the North. These banks have been to a large extent immunized from losses on bad debts by claiming from Northern governments commensurate reductions in the taxation of their profits. But although they have often benefited from such remissions, this has not normally led them to cancel the debt itself. How can it be justified that banks should be compensated for writing down foreign debts, when no such debt is actually annulled? But even when debts burst all social bounds, sliding into mayhem culminating in genocide, international action has proved no easier.

| "Intense ethnic conflict is most often
caused by collective fears of the
future. As groups begin to fear for
their safety . . . conflict becomes
more likely."

AN ETHNIC GROUP'S CONCERN FOR
ITS SURVIVAL CAN LEAD TO CIVIL WAR

David A. Lake and Donald Rothchild

Contrary to popular belief, ethnic conflict does not result from ancient hatreds that are suddenly released by the breakdown of government, argue David A. Lake and Donald Rothchild in the following viewpoint. Instead, they contend that as a government disintegrates, ethnic groups become fearful and anxious about the future. These concerns can easily slide into violence if one group begins to believe that another ethnic group threatens its security, the authors maintain. Lake is a professor of political science at the University of California, San Diego and the research director for international relations at the Institute on Global Conflict and Cooperation in San Diego. Rothchild is a professor of political science at the University of California, Davis.

As you read, consider the following questions:

1. According to the authors, why is competition for scarce resources between different groups an insufficient reason for the occurrence of ethnic violence?
2. What are three common reasons why a group may misrepresent itself, according to Lake and Rothchild?
3. What are some safeguards used in "ethnic contracts" that ensure that one ethnic group is not exploited by another?

Abridged from David A. Lake and Donald Rothchild, "Containing Fear: The Origins and Management of Ethnic Conflict," *International Security*, vol. 2, no. 2 (Fall 1996), pp. 41–75; ©1996 by the President and Fellows of Harvard College and the Massachusetts Institute of Technology. Reprinted by permission of MIT Press. *Footnotes in the original have been omitted in this reprint.*

Since the end of the Cold War, a wave of ethnic conflict has swept across parts of Eastern Europe, the former Soviet Union, and Africa. Localities, states, and sometimes whole regions have been engulfed in convulsive fits of ethnic insecurity, violence, and genocide. Early optimism that the end of the Cold War might usher in a new world order has been quickly shattered. Before the threat of nuclear armageddon could fully fade, new threats of state meltdown and ethnic cleansing have rippled across the international community.

The most widely discussed explanations of ethnic conflict are, at best, incomplete and, at worst, simply wrong. Ethnic conflict is not caused directly by inter-group differences, "ancient hatreds" and centuries-old feuds, or the stresses of modern life within a global economy. Nor were ethnic passions, long bottled up by repressive communist regimes, simply uncorked by the end of the Cold War.

We argue instead that intense ethnic conflict is most often caused by collective fears of the future. As groups begin to fear for their safety, dangerous and difficult-to-resolve strategic dilemmas arise that contain within them the potential for tremendous violence. As information failures and problems of credible commitment . . . take hold, groups become apprehensive, the state weakens, and conflict becomes more likely. Ethnic activists and political entrepreneurs, operating within groups, build upon these fears of insecurity and polarize society. Political memories and emotions also magnify these anxieties, driving groups further apart. Together, these between-group and within-group strategic interactions produce a toxic brew of distrust and suspicion that can explode into murderous violence. . . .

THE CAUSES OF ETHNIC CONFLICT

Most ethnic groups, most of the time, pursue their interests peacefully through established political channels. But when ethnicity is linked with acute social uncertainty, a history of conflict, and fear of what the future might bring, it emerges as one of the major fault lines along which societies fracture. Vesna Pešić, a professor at the University of Belgrade and a peace activist in the former Yugoslavia, says it well: ethnic conflict is caused by the "fear of the future, lived through the past."

Collective fears of the future arise when states lose their ability to arbitrate between groups or provide credible guarantees of protection for groups. Under this condition, which Barry Posen refers to as "emerging anarchy," physical security becomes of paramount concern. When central authority declines, groups become fearful for their survival. They invest in and prepare for violence, and thereby make actual violence possible. State weakness, whether it arises incrementally out of competition between groups or from extremists actively seeking to destroy ethnic peace, is a necessary precondition for violent ethnic conflict to erupt. State weakness helps to explain the explosion of ethnic violence that has followed the collapse of communist regimes in Eastern Europe and the former Soviet Union, and it has also led to violence in Liberia, Somalia, and other African states.

State weakness may not be obvious to the ethnic groups themselves or external observers. States that use force to repress groups, for instance, may appear strong, but their reliance on manifest coercion rather than legitimate authority more accurately implies weakness. More important, groups look beyond the present political equipoise to alternative futures when calculating their political strategies. If plausible futures are sufficiently threatening, groups may begin acting today as if the state were in fact weak, setting off processes, discussed below, that bring about the disintegration of the state. Thus, even though the state may appear strong today, concerns that it may not remain so tomorrow may be sufficient to ignite fears of physical insecurity and a cycle of ethnic violence. The forward-looking nature of the strategic dilemmas emphasized here makes the task of forecasting or anticipating ethnic conflicts especially difficult, both for the participants themselves and external actors who would seek to manage them effectively through preventive diplomacy.

Situations of emerging anarchy and violence arise out of the strategic interactions between and within groups. Between groups, two different strategic dilemmas can cause violence to erupt: information failures and problems of credible commitment. These dilemmas are the fundamental causes of ethnic conflict. Within groups, ethnic activists and political entrepreneurs may make blatant communal appeals and outbid moderate politicians, thereby mobilizing members, polarizing society, and magnifying the inter-group dilemmas. "Non-rational" factors such as emotions, historical memories, and myths can exacerbate the violent implications of these intra-group interactions. Together, these inter-group and intra-group interactions combine, as we explain in this section, to create a vicious cycle that threatens to pull multi-ethnic societies into violence.

STRATEGIC INTERACTIONS BETWEEN GROUPS

Competition for resources typically lies at the heart of ethnic conflict. Property rights, jobs, scholarships, educational admissions, language rights, government contracts, and development allocations all confer benefits on individuals and groups. All such resources are scarce and, thus, objects of competition and occasionally struggle between individuals and, when organized, groups. In societies where ethnicity is an important basis for identity, group competition often forms along ethnic lines.

SETTING THE STAGE FOR ETHNIC VIOLENCE

Serb propagandists began accusing Muslims of preparing to launch a jihad against them. In reality, however, Muslims had no military power and insufficient weapons to consider such a move. The more such projections occurred, the more Bosnian Muslims were perceived, consciously and unconsciously, as Ottoman Turks, the [ancient] enemy [of] the Serbs. The more the Bosnian Muslims' "dangerousness" evolved, the more the Serbs feared them. They also feared a boomerang effect: namely, that their projected aggression would come back to them. Thus, the collective idea that Muslims had to be exterminated began to emerge, and the emotional atmosphere was such that Serbs as a group responded easily to their political and military leaders' manipulations. In fact, these leaders were acting according to the group's existing psychology. The stage was set for the ethnic cleansing of Bosnian Muslims.

Vamik Volkan, Bloodlines: From Ethnic Pride to Ethnic Terrorism, 1997.

Politics matter because the state controls access to scarce resources. Individuals and groups that possess political power can often gain privileged access to these goods, and thus increase their welfare. Because the state sets the terms of competition between groups, it becomes an object of group struggle. Accordingly, the pursuit of particularistic objectives often becomes embodied in competing visions of just, legitimate, and appropriate political orders.

In multi-ethnic societies, resource rivalries and the struggle to control state policy produce competing communal interests. In Nigeria, for example, each ethno-regional group looks to the state to favor it when distributing public resources, producing, as Claude Ake observes, an "overpoliticization" of social life which gravely weakens the state itself. In Yugoslavia, Slovenians and Croatians resented the system of federal redistribution to the poorer regions of the country; their publics backed their leaders' expressions of indignation, ultimately fueling the demand for greater political autonomy. When groups conclude that they can improve their welfare only at the expense of others, they become locked into competitions for scarce resources and state power.

Analytically, however, the existence of competing policy preferences is—by itself—not sufficient for violence to arise. Observers too often fail to recognize this important theoretical point and misattribute violence to competition over scarce resources. Violence, after all, is costly for all communal actors: people are killed; factories, farms, and whole cities are destroyed; resources that might have been invested in new economic growth are diverted instead to destructive ends. As violence, and preparing for violence, is always costly, there must exist in principle some potential bargain short of violence that leaves both sides in a dispute better off than settling their disagreements through the use of force; at the very least, the same *ex post* agreement could be reached without the use of force, and the resources that would have been expended in violence divided somehow between the parties *ex ante*. This holds irrespective of the breadth of the group demands or the extent of the antagonisms. The farther apart the policy preferences of the groups are, the greater the violence necessary for one group to assert its will over the other, and the greater the resources that can be saved by averting the resort to force.

Despite appearances, then, competing policy preferences by themselves cannot explain the resort to violence. The divorce between the two halves of Czechoslovakia is a sterling example of two ethnic groups, in conflict over the distribution of resources within their federal state but anxious to avoid the costs of war, developing a mutually agreeable separation to avoid a potentially violent confrontation. For negotiations to fail to bridge the demands of opposing groups, at least one of three strategic dilemmas must exist. Each dilemma alone is sufficient to produce violent conflict. Nonetheless, they typically occur together as a dangerous syndrome of strategic problems.

INFORMATION FAILURES

Because violence is costly, groups can be expected to invest in acquiring knowledge about the preferences and capabilities of the opposing side and bargain hard, but eventually reach an agreement short of open conflict. Groups might even be expected to reveal information about themselves to prevent violence from erupting. When individuals and groups possess private information and incentives to misrepresent that information, competing group interests can produce actual conflict. We refer to this as an information failure. When information failures occur, groups cannot acquire or share the information necessary to bridge the bargaining gap between themselves, making conflict possible despite its devastating effects.

Incentives to misrepresent private information exist in at least three common circumstances. In each, revealing true information undercuts the ability of the group to attain its interests. First, incentives to misrepresent occur when groups are bargaining over a set of issues and believe they can gain by bluffing. By exaggerating their strengths, minimizing their weaknesses, and mis-stating their preferences, groups seek to achieve more favorable divisions of resources. Through such bluffs, however, they increase the risk that negotiations will fail and conflicts arise.

Second, groups may be truly aggressive but do not want to be branded as such. They may seek to minimize internal opposition, or to insulate themselves from repercussions in the broader international community. Although typically only minimal sanctions are imposed by other states, most groups seek to avoid the label of an aggressor or violator of international norms and the political isolation that such a classification can carry.

Finally, in conflicts where the groups are simultaneously negotiating and preparing for ethnic war, any attempt to facilitate compromise by having each side explain how it plans to win on the battlefield will seriously compromise the likelihood that it will win should war occur. Thus, groups cannot reveal their strategies or derive accurate predictions of their likely success. Paradoxically, each party is bound by its own self-interest to withhold the information crucial to bringing about an agreement. Concerned that private information they provide on how they intend to protect themselves or attack others will redound to their disadvantage, groups may refrain from revealing the information necessary to forge a mutually satisfactory compromise. . . .

PROBLEMS OF CREDIBLE COMMITMENT

Ethnic conflicts also arise because groups cannot credibly commit themselves to uphold mutually beneficial agreements they might reach. In other words, at least one group cannot effectively reassure the other that it will not renege on an agreement and exploit it at some future date. As exploitation can be very costly—up to and including the organized killing of one group by another—groups may prefer to absorb even high costs of war today to avoid being exploited tomorrow.

Stable ethnic relations can be understood as based upon a "contract" between groups. Such contracts specify, among other things, the rights and responsibilities, political privileges, and access to resources of each group. These contracts may be formal constitutional agreements or simply informal understandings between elites. Whatever their form, ethnic contracts channel politics in peaceful directions.

Most importantly, ethnic contracts contain "safeguards" designed to render the agreement self-enforcing. They contain provisions or mechanisms to ensure that each side lives up to its commitments and feels secure that the other will do so as well. Typical safeguards include, first, power-sharing arrangements, electoral rules, or group vetoes that prevent one ethnic group from setting government policy unilaterally; second, minority control over critical economic assets, as with the whites in South Africa or Chinese in Malaysia; and third, as was found in Croatia before the breakup of Yugoslavia, maintenance of ethnic balance within the military or police forces to guarantee that one group will not be able to use overwhelming organized violence against the other. These political checks and balances serve to stabilize group relations and ensure that no group can be exploited by the other. In Barry R. Weingast's words, "reciprocal trust can be induced by institutions.". . .

STRATEGIC INTERACTIONS WITHIN GROUPS

As we have just shown, strategic interactions between groups create the unstable social foundations from which ethnic conflict arises. Information failures and problems of credible commitment . . . demonstrate that even when groups mean well and calculate the costs and benefits of alternatives realistically, conflict can still erupt. Even in "the best of all possible worlds," these strategic dilemmas can produce violent conflict.

Under conditions of actual or potential state weakness, and as the strategic dilemmas described above begin to take hold, two catalysts—ethnic activists and political entrepreneurs—can produce rapid and profound polarization within a multi-ethnic society. Social polarization, in turn, magnifies the strategic dilemmas and potential for conflict described above. As we explain in this section, political memories, myths, and emotions also magnify the polarizing effects of activists and entrepreneurs, further accelerating the vicious cycle of ethnic fear and violence.

All individuals desire to belong to groups, but the strength of this desire differs. In a model of "ethnic dissimilation," Timur Kuran demonstrates that ethnic activists—individuals with especially strong needs to identify with ethnic kin—can manipulate such desires to produce a process of social polarization that is rapid, apparently spontaneous, and essentially unpredictable. By persuading others to increase their public ethnic activity in order to maintain standing within the group, Kuran argues, ethnic activists can drive individuals to represent falsely their true preferences. While they might prefer, for instance, not to associate exclusively with members of their own group, individuals are pressed by activists and the social pressures they spawn to alter their behavior in a more "ethnic" direction. In this way, Kuran finds, ethnic activists can cause previously integrated communities to separate along ethnic lines. . . .

Emotions may also cause individuals and groups to act in exaggerated or potentially "irrational" ways that magnify the chances of conflict. Many analysts point to a deep psychological—perhaps even physiological—need for humans to belong to a group. In the process of drawing distinctions, however, individuals often overstate the goodness of their own group while simultaneously vilifying others. Where such emotional biases exist, groups are likely to interpret the demands of others as outrageous, while seeing their own as moderate and reasonable; to view the other as inherently untrustworthy, while believing themselves to be reliable; to insist upon adequate safeguards against the possible defection of the other, but interpreting the efforts of others to impose similar restrictions on them as a sign of "bad faith"; to believe that the other is withholding information or deceptive, while they are being open and honest; and so on.

The emotional power of ethnic attachments is typically increased by the unifying effects of what are perceived to be external threats. People who have little in common with others may unite when they feel threatened by external enemies. Thus, the shared identity of the Hutu in Burundi emerged only recently with the Tutsi repressions of 1972. Similarly, in Chechnya, when very disparate interests felt threatened by Russian power, they overcame their differences and made common cause in the face of Russian intervention.

Together, strategic interactions between and within groups can produce environments of fear in which ethnic tensions and conflicts can grow. As Pešić recognizes, it is the future that threatens, but the future is interpreted through the past. While each strategic dilemma alone is sufficient to produce and explain the outbreak of ethnic conflict, they almost always occur simultaneously. Ethnic activists and political entrepreneurs can polarize societies, exacerbating these strategic dilemmas. The tendency toward polarization, in turn, is magnified by political memories and myths and emotions. Combined, these forces create a devastating brew of ethnic rivalry and potential violence.

| "When people feel threatened by radical change, . . . a crisis is all that is needed to inflame ethnic war."

MANY FACTORS CAN LEAD TO WAR

Annie Murphy Paul

Annie Murphy Paul argues in the following viewpoint that there are several factors that may trigger an ethnic war. Competition for jobs, food, and political power may set off ethnic violence, she maintains, as may an economic depression or a change in political leadership. Once people feel threatened by some change, Paul asserts, it is relatively easy to arouse panic, fear, and violence in a group. Political leaders also play an important role because they can either stoke or calm the group's panic, she contends. Paul is a news editor for *Psychology Today*.

As you read, consider the following questions:

1. What was the catalyst for bloodshed in Northern Ireland, according to a study cited by Paul?
2. How can the psychology of dysfunctional families be used to understand ethnic conflict, in Paul's opinion?
3. What is terror management theory, according to the author?

Excerpted from Annie Murphy Paul, "Psychology's Own Peace Corps," *Psychology Today*, July/August 1998. Reprinted with permission from *Psychology Today* magazine. Copyright ©1998 (Sussex Publishers, Inc.).

Half a millennium after Columbus realized the world was round, his discovery is just now sinking in. That we're perched on a small piece of an enormous globe is a fact that only people living now have really known—known with the steadiness of pictures beamed to us from satellites, with the clarity of a voice on a cell phone, calling from the other side of the earth.

That awareness can be heady—and for some, unbearably frightening. The great irony of our time is that just as the horizons of globalization are opening wide, so many people are retreating to the dim, close caves of ethnic identity.

They have been "re-tribalized," in the phrase of Daniel Chirot, Ph.D., a sociologist at the University of Washington. He believes that the staggering size and unnerving fluidity of a globalized culture are causing some societies to run for cover, to seek safety and familiarity in the extended family of an ethnic group.

But that hunger for security can quickly turn ugly, as in Bosnia, in Rwanda, in other places where populations have drawn bloodlines that bind them to some and separate them from others.

From a distance, these ethnopolitical conflicts seem to be one frantic, chaotic blur. But is there order to this apparent anarchy? Chirot believes that such conflicts have a logic of their own. He has identified five stages of social organization—from a peaceful, integrated society, to all-out civil war—and has described the conditions that catapult a nation from one stage to the next. His theories could help explain how these conflicts begin—and how they might end.

IDENTITY RUN AMOK

Chirot looks first to history, noting that some of the fiercest ethnic conflicts have occurred in nations that were until recently under the sway of Soviet domination or European colonialism. The withdrawal of these foreign powers left persistent problems, as well as an often-frightening freedom, in its wake.

In some cases, such as the former Yugoslavia, one country split into hostile minority groups. In others, such as Armenia and Azerbaijan, long-standing national enmities re-emerged in the absence of a shared oppressor. "Not only have such passions not lessened, they are now played out on a much larger scale, and involve far more people than in the past," says Chirot.

Many of these repressive regimes imposed a uniform national identity on those they ruled. Russians told members of their republics that they were Soviets first, Latvians or Chechens second.

European conquerors in Africa ignored tribal distinctions, seeing only skin color.

Now that these imperialists have packed their bags, their former subjects are asserting their distinctiveness—with a vengeance. The exaggeration and valorization of difference can reach absurd heights: though the language differences between Croats and Slovenes are slighter than those between Sicilians and Venetians in Italy, for example, the former Yugoslavs believe that they speak different tongues—and each group is convinced that theirs is far superior.

It's no surprise that these long-dominated peoples should choose ethnicity as the vehicle for their newly-liberated identities, says Chirot. Their former, often resented, personas were imposed from without, while ethnicity springs from our very genes.

But the emergence of distinct ethnic groups isn't enough to set off ethnic war, he says. That happens only when people feel that their ethnic group is competing with another one for limited resources—jobs, food, cultural clout. When people feel threatened by radical change, they seek safety in numbers, and any attack on the group is perceived as a personal affront.

Once people are looking through this lens, a crisis is all that is needed to inflame ethnic war. Sometimes the emergency is economic: Chirot observes that a severe recession in Germany in the 1930s propelled the Nazis into power. Fifty years later, economic hard times helped turn Yugoslavia into an ethnic battleground.

But Chirot also notes that other Eastern European countries had rocky economies during the same period, yet did not erupt in civil war. "Economics are a precipitating event, but not a long-run cause," he says. Financial distress simply touches a match to an already brittle political situation.

More often, the crisis is political, a shift in the balance of power between groups that makes both sides nervous. A study that attempted to tie outbreaks of violence in Northern Ireland to the ups and downs of its economy, for example, found no connection between the two. Rather, bloodshed invariably followed changes in the power relationship between Protestants and Catholics.

Ethnic conflict is most likely to occur, Chirot concludes, "when people believe that the other group is going to take power away from them, and that they'll be the long-term losers, in every way: culturally, politically, economically."

Wars Within and Without

As Chirot's investigation of ethnopolitical war moves from such historical and structural conditions into the realms of the mind, certainties are harder to capture. How people think and feel about their ethnicity, about their leaders, about opposing groups, are questions that remain at large.

THE FIVE STAGES OF ETHNIC CONFLICT

1. Multi-ethnic societies without serious conflict. Example: Switzerland.

2. Multi-ethnic societies with conflicts that remain under control and far short of war. Example: United States.

3. Societies where ethnic violence has broken out but has been resolved. Example: South Africa.

4. Societies with serious conflicts that have led to chronic warfare but not genocide. Example: Sri Lanka.

5. Genocidal ethnic conflict, including violent ethnic cleansing. Example: Yugoslavia.

Annie Murphy Paul, *Psychology Today*, July/August 1998.

Psychology would seem to be a natural place to look for answers. But they are surprisingly scarce. Few psychologists have studied either the causes or consequences of ethnic war.

What psychology does have is experience tending to those wounded in the wars within families or within the individual psyche—and that expertise may be directly applicable to ethnic conflict. Knowing what aggravates or soothes tensions in marriage, for example, might prove useful in negotiating between warring factions. Understanding how we project our own fears and hatreds onto other individuals might help us see how that happens on a nationwide scale.

FROM FEAR TO ETERNITY

One of the most basic—and most vexing—questions psychology must answer is how ethnicity becomes such a crucial and closely-held part of people's identities. Ethnicity seems to carry much more weight than other broad groupings, like class or even religion.

A new line of thought in psychology may help explain the strength of ethnicity's grip. Terror management theory, as it's known, tries to understand how we deal with the awareness of our own mortality. It seems that when people are made to think about their own death as they emphatically are when living in an ethnic war zone—they respond by cleaving more closely to some parts of their identity, especially ethnicity. That's because, unlike nationality or religion, ethnicity is passed on biologically to offspring, promising a kind of immortality.

A more unsettling mystery of ethnic conflict is why, once people have embraced their own ethnic group, they so often feel moved to demean and dehumanize the members of other clans. From research on the relations between social groups, psychology offers some clues: excluding and disparaging others may be a way of consolidating one's identity, boosting self-esteem, and bonding more closely with one's own group. But how can these mild-sounding motives account for the slaughter of children in front of their mothers? For women raped and defiled so they will not be able to return to their families?

Perhaps the most puzzling and unpredictable phenomenon psychologists are called upon to explain is panic. Although a real crisis is often the catalyst for ethnic war, that emergency may remain manageable—if it is not accompanied by irrational fear. "If the crisis doesn't provoke a sense of general panic, then reason may remain uppermost and moderates may prevail," says Chirot. "In South Africa, for example, the moderates on both sides seem to have won out."

But sometimes a frenzy of fear and dread will overtake a population, though there may seem to be slight evidence for alarm. The conviction on the part of the various ethnic groups in Yugoslavia that each was out to exterminate the other, for example, was founded on little more than overblown propaganda and outsized suspicions, observes Chirot. Indeed, psychological studies of lynch mobs, urban riots, and cult movements show that people in groups act in ways they never would on their own.

Follow the Leader

They may also be urged on by a charismatic or commanding leader, like Mobutu Sese Seko of Zaire or Radovan Karadzic of Serbia. Here again, psychology can provide some insight. It has produced studies of relatively benign leaders—presidents, principals, CEOs—and psychohistories of more infamous ones like Hitler and Stalin. They may help us understand which qualities persuade people to identify with a leader and what motives drive the leader himself.

Though Chirot concedes that leaders are important, he insists that panic is first aroused in the rank and file. "Leaders can make a panic worse, but there has to be a predisposition to panic," he says. "There has to be something that has gone wrong in people's lives. There has to be a perception of threat."

Leaders can play on that perception, as Adolf Hitler did in his rise to power, or they can debunk it, as Franklin Roosevelt did when he told Americans that they had "nothing to fear but fear itself." More recently, Serbia's Slobodan Milosevic cynically capitalized on the fears of his people of a repeat of World War II, while members of India's government worked hard to dispel tensions between its ethnic factions. Psychology may be able to tell us why leaders go down one path rather than another, and why their supporters follow them there. . . .

Psychology holds out hope for the resolution of ethnic conflict because it's a science of the subjective, a systematic approach to all that is irrational and unpredictable. If it can tame the beast of ethnic conflict, says Chirot, "it will be a great blessing for the world."

PERIODICAL BIBLIOGRAPHY

The following articles have been selected to supplement the diverse views presented in this chapter. Addresses are provided for periodicals not indexed in the *Readers' Guide to Periodical Literature*, the *Alternative Press Index*, the *Social Sciences Index*, or the *Index to Legal Periodicals and Books*.

Robert L. Bartley	"The Road to 'Ethnic Cleansing,'" *Wall Street Journal*, June 11, 1996.
Jay Brophy	"Concerning the 'Troubles' in British-Occupied Ireland," *Turning the Tide*, Fall 1997.
Carole J.L. Collins and Steven Askin	"The Islamic Gulag: Slavery Makes a Comeback in Sudan," *Utne Reader*, March/April 1996.
Mark Danner	"America and the Bosnia Genocide," *New York Review of Books*, December 4, 1997.
Mark Danner	"The U.S. and the Yugoslav Catastrophe," *New York Review of Books*, November 20, 1997.
Seamus Deane	"When Violence Becomes a Habit," *New York Times*, August 18, 1998.
Meg Greenfield	"The Trouble with Tribes," *Newsweek*, July 27, 1998.
Clive Mutiso	"Tribalism: Raising Hope," *Time*, April 13, 1998.
Peace and Democracy	Special section on self-determination, nationalism, and democracy. Spring 1995.
John Pomfret	"Between War and Peace," *Washington Post National Weekly Edition*, December 25–31, 1995. Available from 1150 15th St. NW, Washington, DC 20071.
Richard N. Rosecrance	"The Obsolescence of Territory," *New Perspectives Quarterly*, Winter 1995.
Frederic Paul Smoler	"History's Largest Lessons," *American Heritage*, February/March 1997.
Rupert J. Taylor	"The Warrior Culture," *Canada and the World Backgrounder*, April 1995.

SHOULD THE INTERNATIONAL COMMUNITY INTERVENE IN THE WORLD'S CONFLICTS?

CHAPTER PREFACE

In early 1998, Kosovo, a province within the Yugoslavian republic of Serbia, exploded in violence. Ethnic Albanians, who make up 90 percent of the population of Kosovo, rebelled against the Serb government. The Albanian Kosovars were originally trying to regain their provincial autonomy which had been revoked in 1990 by Yugoslavian president Slobodan Milosevic, but during the early months of the fighting, their desire for autonomy changed into a fight for nationhood. In the fall of 1998, the Serbs, led by Milosevic, gained the advantage in the rebellion, and hundreds of thousands of ethnic Albanians were forced to flee their homes and villages.

The world watched as first Serbians, and then ethnic Albanians, were massacred because of their ethnicity. Some observers argued for intervention—in the form of North Atlantic Treaty Organization (NATO) forces—to stop the violence. They contend that it is unconscionable for the world to stand by and do nothing in the face of mass murder. Genocide, writes author and columnist George F. Will, "trumps concern for Serbia's territorial integrity." Advocates of intervention assert that the NATO forces would protect the Albanians from being the victims of further ethnic cleansing. Moreover, the analysts maintain, the appearance of NATO in the conflict would end the war by forcing Milosevic to negotiate peace with the rebel Kosovars.

Opponents of NATO involvement in Kosovo argue that intervention would break international law by supporting the independence of a legal province of Serbia. Just as the United States went to war to prevent the southern states from seceding during the American Civil War, so too, does Serbia have the right to prevent Kosovo from seceding. Syndicated columnist Charley Reese asks, "What gives the United States the right to tell a sovereign nation how it must react to armed insurrection?" Furthermore, opponents predict that maintaining the peace after NATO intervention is likely to require a long-term occupation of Kosovo, a contingency that most nations are unwilling to accept.

In October 1998, NATO officials, backed by various heads of state, threatened to bomb Yugoslavia and Serbian strongholds unless Milosevic pulled his forces out of Kosovo. The authors in the following chapter debate whether intervention in world conflicts is effective at maintaining peace, and what form that intervention should take.

1

|"It is precisely in these small wars in
faraway places that the United
Nations can make a difference."

INTERVENTION IS EFFECTIVE AT RESTORING PEACE

Lionel Rosenblatt and Larry Thompson

The United Nations (UN) can effectively keep the peace in small, intrastate wars, maintain Lionel Rosenblatt and Larry Thompson in the following viewpoint. However, they assert, the reluctance on the part of member nations to engage in these conflicts necessitates the founding of a standing, permanent international army. This short-term military force would respond quickly to defuse emergency situations until a more long-term peacekeeping force could arrive. Rosenblatt is president of Refugees International, a Washington-based advocacy organization. Thompson is a senior associate with Refugees International.

As you read, consider the following questions:

1. Why did the UN peacekeeping force fail in Rwanda, according to the authors?
2. In the authors' opinion, why does the current UN peacekeeping force need to be supplemented with a rapid response force?
3. Why should the United States support a UN rapid response force, according to Rosenblatt and Thompson?

Excerpted from Lionel Rosenblatt and Larry Thompson, "The Door of Opportunity: Creating a Permanent Peacekeeping Force," *World Policy Journal*, Spring 1998. Reprinted with permission of the *World Policy Journal*.

S omerset Maugham wrote a short story, "The Door of Opportunity," about a British colonial official who was dismissed in disgrace because he lacked the courage to face down a murderous crowd of rioters in some lonely, unimportant corner of the empire. "The utility of a government official depends very largely on his prestige," says the governor to the offender, "and I'm afraid his prestige is likely to be inconsiderable when he lies under the stigma of cowardice."

On the American scene, in John Ford's cavalry classic, *She Wore a Yellow Ribbon*, John Wayne and Ben Johnson, Jr. ride into a hostile Cheyenne village and avert an Indian uprising with a cultural sensitivity that would please a Berkeley don.

Are these two examples of fictional peacekeeping pure myth from a vanished time? Are the people in the age of the AK-47 inherently more dangerous and less amenable to peaceful resolution of conflict than in the black powder era? Or is there some basis to believe that a few good men and women acting with "promptness and firmness" (Maugham's words) can avert some of the uncivil wars and ethnic slaughter that characterize our post–Cold War world?

RWANDA, 1994

Let us look at a contemporary example of a peacekeeping failure: Rwanda, April to August 1994.

On April 6, 1994, an airplane carrying Juvénal Habyarimana, the president of Rwanda, was shot down under mysterious circumstances, setting off a struggle for control of the country between the majority Hutu and minority Tutsi peoples, and the most horrific genocide of the 1990s. Some 800,000 people— mostly Tutsi and moderate Hutus—were killed by Hutu extremists in the space of three months.

Civil war and ethnic violence had been the norm in Rwanda for many years. A lightly armed United Nations (U.N.) peacekeeping force of 2,500 was stationed in the country on a "low-intensity" peacekeeping mission to monitor compliance with a prior agreement between Hutu and Tutsi, a "cakewalk" as one U.N. official said. In the spring of 1994, the flavor of the cake turned out be devil's food. "They [Hutu extremists] were chopping off the breasts of women," said Gen. Romeo Dallaire, the Canadian commander of the U.N. peacekeepers. "They were slitting people open from their genitals right up to their sternum. They were chopping up the arms of two-year-old children just as if it [sic] was salami."

Among early victims were ten Belgian peacekeepers who were

killed on April 7 by Hutu militia. With their deaths, the heart went out of the political masters of the peacekeeping mission in New York and other world capitals, especially Washington.

THE U.N. RESPONSE

General Dallaire had minimal resources at his disposal to contend with the eruption of violence. According to the *Joint Evaluation of Emergency Assistance to Rwanda*, published in 1996, he had only "one working armored personnel carrier, a demoralized Belgian battalion, and an under-equipped, below-strength unit from Bangladesh." Moreover, the peacekeepers had no mandate from the U.N. Security Council to intervene to prevent the mass murders taking place before their eyes. But, in a sign of what might have been had the U.N. force been instructed to protect civilians, 12 "blue helmets" at the Amahoro Stadium, armed only with bluff, hand weapons, and barbed wire, saved the lives of several thousand persons.

The response of Boutros Boutros-Ghali, the U.N. secretary general, and the Security Council to the events in Rwanda was to decide that there was no peace to keep, and on April 21, Boutros-Ghali ordered the withdrawal of most of the peacekeepers. A traumatized Belgium prompted the flight of the United Nations, but a jittery United States, which had recently lost 18 of its own army rangers in Somalia, backed the Belgians. (When the Belgian peacekeepers got back to Brussels, several of them shredded their U.N. blue berets for the television cameras.)

Later, as conscience crept back into the United Nations, Boutros-Ghali proposed a more forceful U.N. role, and the Security Council, including a reluctant and foot-dragging United States, finally approved sending a new peacekeeping force of 5,400 personnel to Rwanda. It was now May 17—six weeks and several hundred thousand lives into the genocide.

TOO LITTLE, TOO LATE

The U.N. Security Council, however, only mandates on paper. Several African countries came forward with offers of troops, but matching ill-equipped African troops with essential Western equipment (to be provided by the United States and other countries) proved to be too much of a bureaucratic obstacle to overcome quickly, given the lack of political will in Western capitals. On July 25, 1994, Boutros-Ghali reported sadly that only 500 of the 5,400 peacekeepers the Security Council had authorized were on the ground in Rwanda and that they were barely operational.

Disgracefully, the first American armored personnel carriers so vital to the success of a U.N. peacekeeping force arrived only on July 30. It was much too little, much too late. The civil war was over. The genocide was over. The United Nations and its members had fiddled for four months while Rwanda burned. The toll in a country of 8 million was astonishing: up to 800,000 people were dead, two million were refugees in neighboring Zaire and Tanzania, and three million were displaced within the country itself. The Rwandan conflict and genocide had a profound impact on Burundi, Uganda, Tanzania, and, especially, Zaire—now the Democratic Republic of Congo—the third largest country of Africa. President Laurent Kabila's rise to power in Congo began with the refugee flight from Rwanda and the spread of the Hutu-Tutsi conflict to eastern Zaire. Perhaps the least important of the consequences was that the international community would be saddled with a tab of half a billion dollars per year to feed the refugees and clean up the mess.

FEAR AND LOATHING OF THE UNITED NATIONS

The political commentator Michael Lind thinks the United Nations and its philosophy of collective security have been "finally and completely discredited" and the organization itself should be allowed to "wither away into irrelevance." Lind argues for a return to nineteenth-century statecraft, in which an ill-defined "great power concert" would run the world. But what, we would ask, will happen if the so-called great powers do not want to run the world? The abdication of responsibility by the great powers in the 1920s and 1930s led to the militaristic rise of Japan, Germany, and Italy. The great powers of the 1990s do not seem to have any more stomach for managing chaos than did France, Britain, or the United States back then.

The scholar David Rieff displays a spirit complementary to Lind's. Rieff discounts the ability of the world to have a positive effect on civil wars and ethnic conflicts. "I would go so far as to suggest that some of these conflicts are inevitable; that they have a certain political logic and also a certain political function; and that in the long run we're actually doing no one any favor by trying to intervene and prevent them."

A synthesis of the writings of the anti–United Nations, anti-intervention theorists might be that "the United Nations is no damn good but even if it were it would have no business sticking its nose into small wars in faraway places to save lives."

We beg to differ. It is precisely in these small wars in faraway places that the United Nations can make a difference. The United Nations is not going to be able to handle a conflict as big as the

1991 Gulf War for the foreseeable future. Even a Bosnia may be too big for the organization to handle. But the United Nations should be equipped to deal with the Liberias, Rwandas, and Macedonias of the world—with the chaos, ethnic conflicts, or threats of strife in countries that do not engage the urgent political concerns of the big powers: a few hundred thousand dead people here, a few hundred thousand there, add up.

It seems to us not too much to ask that the international community regard the preservation of lives as an important factor when it deliberates about intervention in crisis situations. We should be hardheaded; but we should nor be coldhearted.

THE FAILURE OF A PEACEKEEPING MISSION

International peacekeeping failed in Rwanda for several reasons. First, the U.N. peacekeeping force at the outbreak of the genocide was a mixed bag of soldiers from several countries, indifferently equipped and trained, inadequately financed, and barely coordinated because each national military unit ultimately looked to its own chain of command for orders rather than to the nominal commander, General Dallaire.

Second, the terms of reference for the peacekeeping force were all wrong. It was, to quote the *Joint Evaluation*, "a classic, minimalist peacekeeping operation," with no authority to protect innocent lives if the uneasy peace between Tutsi and Hutu it was supervising broke down. In fact, there was no option for action at all in case of trouble except withdrawal. With no peace to keep, the Security Council withdrew the peacekeepers.

Third, national considerations took precedence over the needs of the U.N. peacekeeping mission and the people of Rwanda. When the Belgian peacekeepers were brutally killed, the Belgian government decided immediately to withdraw its forces. The United States seconded Brussels, partially because of a penny-pinching attitude about peacekeeping worthy of Ebenezer Scrooge. (The U.N. peacekeeping mission to Rwanda cost the United States about $5 million per month; the failure of the peacekeeping mission would ultimately cost U.S. taxpayers $125 million in less than a month for an emergency military airlift to feed Rwandan refugees.) The French intervened unilaterally in southwestern Rwanda (Operation Turquoise). Although the French intervention undoubtedly saved some lives, it also reflected mixed political and humanitarian motives and helped the Hutu army and militia, the primary perpetrators of the bloodbath, remain intact.

Suppose a well-trained, well-equipped U.N. peacekeeping force had been in Rwanda when war broke out in April 1994. And suppose that it had had a mandate to protect civilian lives. Could such a force have stemmed the ensuing genocide and its many tragic aftershocks? Dallaire thinks so. "Had we been able to deploy the troops and equipment with a mandate to prevent a situation of crimes against humanity and to be more offensive in nature, I believe we could have curtailed a significant portion of it."

THE RIGHT AND OBLIGATION TO INTERVENE

Increasing numbers of people are willing to act on what must be an implicit belief that sovereignty does not reside with an abstraction called the state, and certainly not with self-appointed military or civilian dictatorships, but with the people of a country themselves. Even more, the view seems to hold, the power of all governments, even those popularly elected, is limited: individuals have inalienable rights that must be observed and protected by all governments. As a result, according to this increasingly powerful view, all governments can be held to certain standards of behavior involving basic human rights and democratic processes. In addition, when a country falls into such disarray that no governing body can end a humanitarian tragedy, the world community itself is accountable. When such events occur, the view continues, all people in other countries, and their governments, have not only the right, but the obligation, to intervene on behalf of both oppressed peoples and innocent bystanders.

Barry M. Blechman, *Washington Quarterly*, Summer 1995.

Dallaire goes on to pinpoint the U.N.'s number-one problem in its peacekeeping operations. "The United Nations is not a sovereign state with the resources of a sovereign state. It can take decisions but it has to go outside to get resources, particularly troops and equipment. When I left at the end of August 1994, I had barely 3,000 of the [promised] 5,500 troops."

Dallaire's words lead us to a proposal that is gaining currency in international circles: to create a standing, permanent, international rapid response force to deal with situations like the one in Rwanda.

A RAPID REACTION FORCE

The secretary general's "Supplement to an Agenda for Peace" in January 1995 called on the United Nations to consider the idea of a "rapid deployment force." Denmark and Belgium, mindful of the tragedy in Rwanda, are behind the idea; Canada lends support; and even the United States—reluctant though it may be—has come up with a variation on the theme: an African Crisis Response Initiative of 5,000–10,000 African troops, internationally trained and financed, to respond to crises on the continent.

The present system of international peacekeeping is too slow, too cumbersome, too inefficient, too prone to failure, too ad hoc to meet the necessities of the confusing, nameless era that has followed in the wake of the Cold War. Former U.N. under secretary general Brian Urquhart says the United Nations is at the "sheriff's posse" stage. "There are a lot of people who don't really agree with each other very much most of the time who suddenly are shocked by some horrendous human event into putting together some ad hoc and improvised posse to do something about it after the fact. It is better than doing nothing, of course. But we've got to move on from this stage." For one thing, the world body is too slow and unprofessional to create and mobilize a "sheriff's posse" whenever the need arises.

STEPS TOWARD IMPROVEMENTS

Stung by its failure in Rwanda, the United Nations has taken some steps toward improving its peacekeeping capabilities. U.N. headquarters in New York now has a 24-hour watch center to monitor crises around the world. A rapidly deployable headquarters team is being formed to assess crises early on, before peacekeeping forces are sent out. The Standby Arrangement System maintains a register of personnel and equipment volunteered by member states that can be utilized for peacekeeping missions. Planning, intelligence, and early warning functions have been enhanced.

All this may be superfluous if, when the necessity for deployment of peacekeepers arises, as it does suddenly, the need for troops and matériel cannot be met. "Unconditional commitments" of aid from member states have a way of evaporating when the United Nations calls in the chits. Domestic politics tends to govern the response of member states to an urgent demand for peacekeeping. National pride, particularly that of the French and the Americans, complicates command and control. The French do not work well with anybody, and the Americans will not work at all unless they are in charge.

TIME IS CRITICAL

Time is a critical factor. Opportunities to defuse a situation are lost in the time between a Security Council decision and the actual deployment of troops on the ground. Dallaire needed reinforcements in Rwanda in April—not in August.

The best solution to these problems would seem to be the creation of a standing, permanent international military and police force made up of volunteers and under the direct command of the U.N. Security Council: what has variously been called a rapid reaction force (RRF), a rapid deployment brigade, a U.N. foreign legion. . . .

What would a rapid reaction force do? First, it would be available to reinforce long-term U.N. peacekeeping missions on an emergency basis. For example, if events turned sour in Cyprus or Macedonia, a battalion or two from the RRF could be sent out to reinforce the existing U.N. peacekeeping forces in those countries. RRF deployments would be temporary, not to exceed six months in most cases. Either the crisis would be resolved during those six months or a long-term peacekeeping force would be assembled. The elite troops of the RRF should not end up walking the Green Line in Cyprus for 20 years. . . .

GETTING BIG DADDY ON BOARD

Canada, Denmark, and the Netherlands have taken [the international community's failure to prevent genocide] to heart in proposing means by which the United Nations can deploy peacekeepers more rapidly and efficiently than at present. All the rhetoric in the world, however, is not going to result in the creation of a rapid reaction force unless the big daddy on the international scene, the United States of America, gets behind the idea. Penuriousness, neo-isolationism, and hostility toward the United Nations are holding it back.

Yet, a rapid reaction force has much to recommend itself to the United States. First, if a competent, international peacekeeping force existed, the need for U.S. bilateral deployment, as in Somalia and Haiti would decrease, thereby reducing America's costs and casualties. Second, the anguished political debate that arises at the prospect of U.S. soldiers being sent in harm's way would be stilled. (American volunteers, we foresee, might serve in an RRF, but they would be outside the jurisdiction and responsibility of the Department of Defense.) And, third, with such a force under the control of the Security Council, the United States would always be able to use its veto if it did not approve of a proposed deployment. . . .

IN AMERICA'S BEST INTERESTS

The occasional necessity for international peacekeeping forces is doubted by virtually nobody. With the states of Central Africa in turmoil and the Bosnian situation far from settled, to name just two areas of concern, the question we must ask ourselves is whether the present ad hoc system of international peacekeeping is the best possible mechanism. The answer is an emphatic no. The creation of a rapid reaction force would give the international community the means to prevent and contain conflicts and to protect noncombatants that it now sadly lacks.

The United States should promote the creation of a rapid reaction peacekeeping force. It is in America's own interest to quiet the brushfires of distant conflicts before they burn out of control.

"No peacekeeper who has intervened in a communal conflict has yet been able to withdraw after successfully restoring peace between the combatants."

INTERVENTION IS FREQUENTLY INEFFECTIVE

Joseph R. Rudolph Jr.

Most peacekeeping ventures—whether undertaken by the United Nations or by individual countries—have been unable to restore peace permanently to war-torn areas so that the peacekeepers could withdraw, argues Joseph R. Rudolph Jr. in the following viewpoint. He contends that peacekeeping interventions are generally unsuccessful because ethnic conflicts are inherently explosive and because the peacekeepers often take sides—or appear to take sides—in the conflict. Furthermore, Rudolph maintains, peacekeeping often fails because the intervening countries are unsure of their role as peacekeepers and uncertain how to resolve the conflict. Rudolph is a professor of political science at Towson State University in Maryland and the author of several articles and a book on ethnic conflict.

As you read, consider the following questions:

1. What examples does Rudolph present to support his contention that peacekeepers are unable to withdraw after establishing peace between warring factions?
2. What are three obstacles that inevitably prevent a successful peacekeeping intervention, according to Rudolph?
3. In the author's view, how have peacekeeping forces tended to define their mission?

Excerpted from Joseph R. Rudolph Jr., "Intervention in Communal Conflicts," *Orbis*, Spring 1995. Reprinted by permission of JAI Press. Footnotes in the original article have been omitted in this reprint.

One of the most rapidly growing developments in international relations is the involvement of third-party peacekeepers in communal conflicts. Whether undertaken by a country within the framework of quasi-domestic policy (Britain in Northern Ireland), by states assisting overextended clients or asserting regional hegemony (the United States in Lebanon and India in Sri Lanka), or by international organizations seeking to defuse regional disputes (the United Nations in Cyprus, Lebanon, and Yugoslavia), third-party intervention has become one of the more common conflict-management activities of our time. Yet, in theaters of communal conflict it has also been an almost entirely unrewarding activity. *No peacekeeper who has intervened in a communal conflict has yet been able to withdraw after successfully restoring peace between the combatants.* United Nations troops skill patrol the corridor between Greek and Turkish Cypriots and are skill in Beirut; British troops remain in Ulster a generation after their deployment. Where the peacekeepers have departed—the Indian army from Sri Lanka, British troops from interwar Palestine, American forces from Lebanon—the conflict has continued.

This pattern, whose recent replication in Bosnia, Rwanda, and elsewhere has dampened earlier enthusiasm for interventionary diplomacy in the post–cold war world, seems not to result from personal and organizational failure on the part of the peacekeeper. Rather, it seems to derive from the explosiveness of communal politics; a trio of chronically present, perhaps inherently fatal, obstacles to success awaiting those enmeshed in communal peacekeeping operations; and a peacekeeping model woefully out of synchronization with the peacekeeping operations currently being undertaken.

THE EXPLOSIVENESS OF COMMUNAL CONFLICT

The potential for communal conflict is widespread; the possibilities for peacefully resolving communal disputes are few.

Of the states in today's world, less than a third can be labeled nation-states, composed of a mono- or multi-ethnic political community whose members overwhelmingly identify with one another as a nation and with the government as their government. In the remainder, multiple, politically self-differentiating communities coexist within the same borders, with identities that, according to Fred W. Riggs, "antedate territorial states" and rest "consciously or unconsciously [on] shared complexes of . . . symbols, values and norms." Typically, these communities are rooted in ethnic identities kept alive by differences in language, religion, and perhaps physical appearance, and a previous history of mutual antagonism towards one another. Ethnic self-differentiation, in turn, often gives rise to the drive for political autonomy that Walker Connor refers to as ethno-nationalism. Frequently, writes Rupert Emerson, "the determination that a nation exists can effectively be made only after the fact when the nation has emerged full-blown and leaves little reasonable doubt that it is there and must be reckoned with." Yet, even when a community has not evolved a sense of national identity demanding political self-determination, communal conflict can generate great emotion and violence.

Peacemaking in so volatile a climate is inevitably a high-risk undertaking. Several scholars argue that it may not be a feasible one where the nation is still largely based on cultural, historical, and religious identity rather than on where a person lives (the focus of the Western *jus soli* concept of nation [in which one's country of birth determines one's citizenship]). Certainly the problems generated by the differences separating such communities have seldom been easily managed by domestic political processes. . . .

THE DIFFICULTIES OF CONFLICT RESOLUTION

In international as in domestic politics, conflicts of interest are most readily settled whenever the aggrieved party can be appeased without the security of others being jeopardized. In instances of communal conflict, however, it is sometimes difficult to find genuine and objective interests susceptible to negotiation. "Wronged" groups often want compensation for past injustices as well as redress of immediate complaints, while the (once) dominant groups fear that conceding any ground will only stimulate the appetites of those mistreated in the past.

The opportunity for conflict resolution further diminishes where: (1) the majorities and minorities are too intermingled to permit a viable territorial or federal partition (for example, in Bosnia); (2) the majority can envision itself as a minority within a broader context (as with Northern Ireland's Protestants, who, although a two-thirds majority in Ulster, would constitute less than a quarter of the population in an integrated Ireland); and (3) outside parties have become involved in the struggle (as in Lebanon, Northern Ireland, and Cyprus). . . .

THE PROBLEM OF APPEARING NEUTRAL

Retaining the appearance of neutrality is perhaps the crucial element in peacekeeping; however, with the exception of U.N. personnel in Cyprus, peacekeepers in areas of communal violence have been unable to do so. Instead, peacekeepers have fallen into a cyclical pattern of failure: involvement in the conflict results in estrangement from at least one of the combatting parties; that estrangement, in turn, causes the mission to collapse.

The 1969 dispatch of British troops to Northern Ireland and the 1982 arrival of American troops in Beirut were initially greeted with relief by the communities in those areas. Northern Ireland's Protestants viewed the arriving British troops as strengthening Ulster's membership in the United Kingdom, while Catholics saw them as a source of protection from the Protestant-dominated Ulster police. In Lebanon, Christians perceived the Americans as, ultimately, their allies. At the same time, most Muslim factions, although less enchanted with the arrival of the Americans, viewed their deployment as a useful restraint on the Israelis and protection against further grievance-settling massacres by the warring factions inside Beirut. Nevertheless, in both instances, the troops soon became identified with a particular side.

NORTHERN IRELAND

In Northern Ireland, the 1970–72 use of the troops to enforce regional laws (especially the unpopular curfew acts) gradually alienated the British soldiers from the Catholic community and identified them with the region's Protestant-Unionist majority. As a result, well before the "Bloody Sunday" incident of January 1972, when the troops fired into a crowd of demonstrating Catholic civilians, British peacekeepers had become targets of Irish Republican Army assassins. Shortly thereafter, the suspension of Ulster's civilian government alienated British troops from the Protestant majority as well, especially when London made it clear that the restoration of home rule would only occur in a bi-communal, power-sharing framework.

LEBANON

Image was likewise fatal to America's 1982–83 peacekeeping operations in Beirut. Marines who were stationed there indicate that almost immediately after their deployment the environment changed from passive to threatening as the Muslim communities concluded that the troops had come to help the Christian forces, who were in fact being trained by Americans. By January 1983, American marines had become the targets of snipers; after the April attack on the U.S. embassy, incidents involving American troops escalated sharply.

On September 19, American naval forces were ordered to respond to these developments by providing support for the

(Christian) Lebanese armed forces defending the high ground over the marines' position. Opposed by the marine commander in Beirut, the action took the United States across the delicate boundary separating peacekeeping from direct involvement in Lebanon's conflict. The bombing of the marines' quarters and the simultaneous explosion at the headquarters housing French peacekeeping forces came less than five weeks later, effectively ending U.S. peacekeeping operations in Lebanon....

Reprinted by permission of Chuck Asay and Creators Syndicate.

The United Nations has done better in retaining the image of neutrality necessary for peacekeeping troops to function, although it is fair to note that the United Nations begins in the Third World with a more neutral image than most of the major powers. It has also often benefitted from being called into a situation only after the third-party services of others have failed (after the British in Cyprus, after European Union attempts to broker the Yugoslav civil war). There have thus been fewer unrealistic expectations surrounding U.N. efforts. Most important, its peacekeeping forces have tended to operate within guidelines that limit their involvement in a conflict and that have generally confined their peacekeeping operations to certain monitoring functions or the patrolling of buffer zones between rival countries and communities. Where these buffer zones have not existed, however, even the United Nations has had difficulty protecting its image. Thus, its largely successful operation in Cyprus stands in sharp contrast to its ventures in Lebanon, Yugoslavia, and Somalia, where its forces have found themselves entrapped in civil wars fought largely in cities or regions composed of intermingled, warring communities.

The Lebanon operation has been essentially a holding operation since the 1983 attacks on the American and French peacekeeping forces in Beirut. The United Nations has had only limited success in facilitating the quest for peace among factions that are not particularly interested in negotiating. Meanwhile, events in Yugoslavia, especially in Bosnia-Herzegovina, have unfolded much more along Lebanese than Cypriot lines. Whatever the impressions of the battle-weary civilian communities in Bosnia may have been when U.N. forces were deployed during the winter of 1991–92, U.N. peacekeepers had little success in maintaining a neutral position vis-à-vis the region's contending armies. To the Serbian military factions, the U.N. forces posed a threat to their ability to consolidate and expand their territorial gains in Muslim districts. The Muslim factions, though inclined to see the peacekeepers in the short term as benefactors, opposed U.N.-guaranteed cease-fire lines and plans that prevented them from regaining land they had lost. By summer 1992, the U.N. forces were under frequent fire from one side or another somewhere in Bosnia-Herzegovina; when the focus shifted to achieving a cease-fire in and around Sarajevo, the attacks accelerated.

THE U.N. AS PART OF THE CONFLICT

Two years later, the tale remained essentially unchanged, with Serbian spokesmen repeatedly threatening dire consequences to U.N. field personnel should air strikes be ordered against Serbian artillery positions and the Bosnian Muslims demanding the court-martial of the commander of the United Nations's twenty-three thousand forces for his "pro-Serbian" actions. Whether the advancing armies were Bosnian Muslims (their October 1994 offensive) or Serbian (the November 1994 counteroffensive), the status of the U.N. forces remained the same. Far from being neutral buffers, they had become obstacles to effective, communal military operations and, hence, a part of the conflict—much as occurred in the quasi-communal, clan-warfare environment of Somalian politics. There, in 1993, the United Nations responded to attacks on its personnel by launching offensive activities against one of Somalia's contending factions. Nor was this the only parallel between the U.N. operations in Somalia and Bosnia by the end of 1994. In both instances, at least as much consideration was being given to the problem of safely withdrawing U.N. forces as to the means for enhancing their effectiveness.

This checkered history of peacekeeping operations is partially attributable to the fact that in many of these "peacekeeping" ventures, the intervening parties were not neutral when they launched the operation or capable of being perceived as neutral for very long. The United States had a definite stake in the outcome of the communal conflict in Lebanon [and] Britain in Northern Ireland. . . .

PEACEKEEPING OBSTACLES

Nevertheless, the greater obstacles to retaining a neutralist position in these conflicts have resulted from the absence of a shared desire on the part of the fighting parties for a cease-fire (finding a peace to keep); the intermingled nature of the communities (which denies peacekeepers a clear cease-fire boundary to maintain even if that desire exists); and, most important, the manner in which the peacekeepers have viewed their role.

Unilateral and multilateral peacekeeping personnel alike have tended to define their mission in communal conflicts in legal terms (for example, the breakdown of laws needing enforcing) or military terms (forces contending for territory). Choosing either set of terms means *identifying with the status quo* in a dynamic situation, an inherently fatal peacekeeping error. The fundamental problem in communal conflicts is that it is the legitimacy of the status quo that is at issue. To identify with it means, however inadvertently or indirectly, breaching the line separating peacekeeping from siding with the established governing arrangement, or with one of the forces competing for influence. . . .

THE ABSENCE OF A WORKABLE MODEL

Finally, conflict management and conflict resolution efforts have suffered alike from an absence of clearly defined agendas and models for peacekeeping (the "what are we going to do here" issue) and conflict resolution (the "what can ultimately be done" conundrum).

Street mediation is the basic, day-to-day task of peacekeeping intervention. Unlike ordinary military activities, peacekeeping operations seek to restore or create a civil community. Basic military training is thus unlikely to provide sufficient preparation for communal peacekeeping duties. Nonetheless, peacekeeping personnel have been drawn overwhelmingly from the military and then asked to function as combination policemen-diplomats, usually without special training for the physical or psychological demands of the job. Only the United Nations has developed a structural framework that defines troop responsibilities to include routine performance of community service activities and customarily uses troops explicitly trained for peacekeeping ventures. This training, however, may soon be curtailed as Canada and other countries that have long contributed contingents reconsider their commitments in light of the United Nations's growing number of operations in highly dangerous areas. Furthermore, even these training arrangements can only partially prepare peacekeeping units.

Prior to 1992, U.N. peacekeeping missions overwhelmingly involved such small-scale and relatively low-risk tasks as monitoring cease-fires, observing troop withdrawals, and patrolling borders and buffer zones. As a consequence, six of the twenty-seven peacekeeping missions that the United Nations undertook between 1947 and 1992 required fewer than a hundred peacekeepers, and sixteen functioned with less than a thousand. Only five were intermediate-sized undertakings requiring between four thousand and six thousand troops, and only one—the disastrous Congo operation—required more. By contrast, since 1992 there have already been three operations comparable to the twenty-thousand troops committed to the Congo (Bosnia, Somalia, and Cambodia), and two of these have been high-risk, communal peacekeeping ventures. Yet even if Canada and others traditionally training forces for peacekeeping operations continue to do so, their training arrangements can at best only partially prepare the peacekeeping forces for the challenges awaiting them.

The frequently drawn analogy between the role of the international peacekeeper and that of the foot policeman who mediates neighborhood conflicts is not only anachronistic but dangerously faulty, for the concept of "neighborhood" suggests a type of consensus absent in inter-communal strife. Meanwhile, the growing number and diversity of peacekeeping operations—from patrolling borders, to tendering humanitarian relief, to defending besieged minorities—can make the experience gained in one operation poor preparation for deployment into another. So, too, can the diversity of the communal conflicts themselves—from the cold-bloodedness of the Northern Ireland conflict to the runaway violence of the tribal warfare in Rwanda. . . .

PEACEKEEPING INTERVENTION AND THE NATIONAL INTEREST

The frustrations that result (at least in part) from oversimplifying the nature of peacekeeping operations have recently led to diminished support for peacekeeping missions in general, even though the recent setbacks have essentially involved only communal peacekeeping ventures, the most difficult of all peacekeeping operations. As a result of these setbacks, the United States and others are less likely to be co-opted into future peacekeeping operations, even though their presence may be essential to the success of these ventures. Likewise, the cost of the current operations measured in terms of money and lives is forcing Canada and other traditional suppliers of peacekeeping forces to reconsider their commitments, leaving a void that cannot be filled by the ill-trained troops of ex-Soviet bloc and Third World states eager to sell their services for hard currency. Yet, however understandable it may be, this growing aversion to peacekeeping may prove shortsighted and dangerous. For not all peacekeeping operations involve communal conflict, while even those that do (as Cyprus attests) can sometimes be limited to low-hazard monitoring of long-term truces. Likewise, as Alan James has cautioned, peacekeeping operations should not be assessed solely on the basis of whether the conflict is resolved but also on the degree to which they forestall escalation and otherwise contribute to the preservation of life and property.

Automatic rejection of communal peacekeeping activity is as unjustified as conscious selectivity and caution are essential. In any case, third-party peacekeeping has already become the extra-systemic response of choice for managing conflicts that cannot be resolved by means of the accommodation devices common to the developed Western world. So, we can expect to hear continued calls for peacekeeping operations, especially given the recent resurgence of tribalism in Africa and the continued strength of nationalism and irredentism inside much of the former Soviet Union and Eastern Europe. . . .

Cost-Benefit Analysis

Responding to these pressures through the prudent use of peacekeeping and other forms of interventionary diplomacy will be among the important challenges of the present decade. Yet, for all the talk of the new world order and post-Soviet world, the conflicts of today's world order pose only slightly different questions to American foreign policy than yesteryear's. Does a given conflict warrant action? Is it occurring in such an important area of the world, or causing such grievous injury that it calls for a response? If the conflict requires a response, is the United Nations or some other multilateral framework the proper medium for that action, and is peacekeeping the proper tool for answering the threat? And, lastly, how costly is the action likely to be, and do the gains of involvement justify those costs?

Where the situation involves geopolitically significant areas, relatively low levels of violence, or unconscionably high levels of destruction, peacekeeping intervention even in communal conflicts may still pass a cost-benefit analysis. But knee-jerk interventionism, multilateral or otherwise, is surely a prescription for disaster—if not on the scale of Vietnam, at least on that of Lebanon or Somalia. That is to say: look before you leap.

| "Private citizens represent an untapped resource for effective humanitarian intervention."

PRIVATE CITIZENS SHOULD INTERVENE TO RESTORE PEACE

Paul Wehr

In the following viewpoint, Paul Wehr maintains that in the past private citizens have played an important role intervening in violent confrontations. The armed forces are ineffective at interventions, he asserts, because they frequently practice violence, and the peace they negotiate is often the result of coercion rather than persuasion. Wehr argues that with appropriate training in conflict resolution, citizen intervenors can reduce violence in the world's conflicts. Wehr is an associate professor of sociology at the University of Colorado in Boulder and the author of *The Persistent Activist*.

As you read, consider the following questions:

1. According to Wehr, what movements were behind the expansion of citizen intervention during the 1980s?
2. What are some global forces that may discourage citizen intervention, according to the author?
3. What examples does the author give of safeguards that may be required to ensure that citizen intervenors are trained properly?

Reprinted from Paul Wehr, "The Citizen Intervenor," *Peace Review*, vol. 8, no. 4 (December 1996), p. 555, by permission.

In the wake of the Somalian, Rwandan and Bosnian crises, and on the brink of the Burundi conflict, we should consider not whether the outside world should intervene to moderate civil violence in such cases, but how it should do so. Governments and nongovernmental organizations (NGOs) quite simply must expand the world's capacity to protect civilians from violence, whether internal or external.

Military institutions, whose past interventions have usually been aggressive, now sometimes seek socially useful and ethically justifiable missions. There is certainly a role for them, interposing themselves to prevent armed conflict, as they currently do in Bosnia. U.N. and regional peacekeeping forces are muddling through similar missions in Liberia and Haiti.

GOOD INTENTIONS UNDERMINED

For several reasons, however, humanitarian military intervention undermines its good intentions in practice. First, military forces are popularly perceived more as the perpetrators rather than the deterrents of violence against civilians. Bosnia, Chechnya, and Rwanda are only the most recent contemporary historical instances that come to mind.

Second, the success of armed intervention, regardless of intentions, depends primarily on the threat or actual use of force. Such methods coerce rather than persuade. In the longer run, they produce fear and instability rather than security and stability. Even with the most favorable conditions and benevolent intentions, armed humanitarian intervention can only succeed in the short term. With time, the temptation to use greater force overcomes caution, as indigenous resistance to the external presence inevitably escalates.

Third, the inexorable trend toward more remote and destructive weapons further removes military forces from the caution, nuance and sensitivity so necessary for a successful humanitarian intervention. Given the limits imposed by the nature and purpose of military institutions, their role in humanitarian interventions must necessarily be a limited one.

Of course, non-military intervention also exists. Diplomacy provides an example, although it is more often used in conjunction with threats to use military force. Another example is the humanitarian relief agency, which usually works independent of military force. When it does associate too closely with the military, its effectiveness quickly diminishes, as we saw with U.N. involvement in Somalia and Bosnia.

Can we develop other, more effective forms of non-military

humanitarian intervention? Arguably, yes. Private citizens represent an untapped resource for effective humanitarian intervention. Their disciplined and structured participation could supplement and enhance the established agents of intervention. Actually, the tradition of the citizen intervenor (CI) in human history is a long and notable one; thus, we need not start from scratch. That tradition has already produced an organizational base around the world that could be better mobilized to reduce violence across national boundaries in the 21st century.

A SOLID TRADITION

For nearly two centuries, peace activists have assumed that "peace is too important to be left to the experts." Citizen efforts to advise those experts can be traced back at least to William Penn's prototypical charter for a European peace zone, a document he modestly shared with heads of state in the 17th century. The tradition of civilian intervention as peacemakers grew substantially in the 19th century. Elihu Burritt's life-long campaign for an international peace regime included his extended residence in Western Europe capitals as a citizen lobbyist. Such early interventions were often welcomed by governments.

By the 20th century, lay peacemakers found their efforts less well received. Heads of government usually dismissed them out of hand. Jane Addams and her coworkers in the Women's International League for Peace and Freedom labored mightily to deter World War I. But as citizen intervenors they were rebuffed, even vilified for meddling in "affairs of state." They were women, bad enough. They were ordinary citizens, worse yet. Woodrow Wilson found them annoying, to say the least, and Theodore Roosevelt thought them "dangerous."

Since World War II, direct intervention across national borders by NGOs and individuals to relieve suffering and deter violence has grown significantly. Post-war reconstruction and work camp programs such as those of the Quaker and Mennonite service organizations were models for later governmental programs like the Peace Corps, the Scandinavian development agencies and the French "cooperants." My own experience as a Quaker "intervenor" in such a program during the Algerian Revolution marked me greatly, setting me firmly on a life path of conflict scholarship and peace action.

Usually such civilian initiatives have had official blessing but occasionally, as when U.S. Quakers delivered evenhanded humanitarian aid to both North Vietnam and South Vietnam in the 1960s, they have met governmental condemnation and punishment. Gradually, citizens in organizations such as Amnesty International, *Medecins sans Frontieres* [Doctors Without Borders], and Sister Cities International have assumed a major responsibility for reducing violence across national borders. As we move into a new century, there's a solid tradition, and at least some governmental acceptance, for the civilian's right and responsibility to intervene.

EXPANSION

That tradition expanded in the 1980s, from an explosive growth in citizens claiming the right to participate in transnational humanitarian intervention. Two movements in particular—nuclear pacifism and Central American solidarity—produced some important citizen experiments. A Women's Walk for Nuclear Disarmament moved for months through Northern European nations, meeting many citizens and government leaders. In the Americas, numerous caravans with humanitarian aid went from North America to El Salvador and Nicaragua despite harassment from hostile governments along the way.

Witness for Peace and Peace Brigades International developed the practice of protective presence. Their multinational teams would live, work and travel with Central Americans at risk—human rights activists, coffee harvesters, border villagers. The simple presence of foreigners—particularly U.S. Americans—was thought to be a deterrent to armed attack.

Some communities intervened through city twinning. Boulder, Colorado, for example, linked with Dushanbe in the Soviet Union and Jalapa in Nicaragua. Reciprocal visitations and cultural exchanges have developed from those projects that have outlived both the Cold War and the Contra War. An elementary school in Jalapa and a Tadjikistani tea house in Boulder are lasting monuments to that citizen intervention.

The Carter Center initiatives provide another, unusual example of citizen diplomacy. Jimmy Carter is, of course, a citizen with special status and experience. Still, his intervention as a private mediator in international crises in Haiti, Bosnia, Nicaragua, and North Korea has produced ambivalence and sometimes hostility among professional diplomats. Nevertheless, Carter's efforts have promoted the cause of direct private citizen involvement in transnational peacemaking.

CONFLICT RESOLUTION TRAINING

Further developments have come in the last few years. First, regional and local leaders from areas of great tension are being trained in conflict moderation methods, and linked together through interorganizational networks. London-based International Alert, for example, has developed a crisis management network, linking regionally with groups like the Coordinating Committee for Conflict Resolution Training in Europe. Other networks have grown out of university programs, at Uppsala and George Mason, for example, and have trained scores of young professionals from the developing world in conflict management. Likewise, the Global Commission to Fund the U.N. has pressured the Security Council to form Anticipatory Risk-Mitigation Peace-Building Contingents, which would provide an "in-place, on-call network of professionals already engaged in [trust-building, reconstruction, conflict resolution, risk mitigation and confidence building] activities in many countries." They would be a resource for the peace-building function the U.N. peacekeeping forces cannot perform.

VOLUNTEERS CAN MAKE A DIFFERENCE

Mediation and conflict resolution provide additional techniques that volunteers can use to make an amazing difference in helping prevent war, especially if they are used early, before fighting breaks out. . . .

[Three volunteer mediators] were able to bring together four Romanian government officials and four representatives of Romania's Hungarian minority for talks that produced a peaceful settlement to diffuse growing ethnic tensions. . . . This may well have prevented another war like that in former Yugoslavia. . . .

The cost of mediation was about one million times less than the cost of a military intervention, yet it was much more successful, saving many lives. This speaks strongly for early, non-military intervention, whenever possible.

Dietrich Fischer, *Peace Review*, December 1996.

The peace team movement has also been active in the 1990s, training citizens with religious and humanitarian motivations in crisis settings. According to Elise Boulding, it includes faith-based groups—the Quakers, the Mennonites, the Swedish Life and Peace Institute, the World Council of Churches—and secular organizations, in a network of about 50 groups. In recent years, exploratory peace teams have been sent to crisis zones in Bosnia, Haiti, and the Persian Gulf, revealing both the potential and the barriers of private intervention.

A related outgrowth has been the increasing demand by NGOs for more citizen participation in the U.N. This has included proposals for a people's counterpart of the General Assembly, which would also sponsor parallel intervention efforts in the field.

Citizen intervention against war and violence also has an academic track. Peace and conflict study and research have deepened the conviction that knowledgeable citizens can learn to reduce violence in our conflicts. Scholars know a lot about peace and justice activism, about moderating conflict, and about non-violent action for self-defense and social change. The development of the International Peace Research Association, and peace and conflict sections in social science organizations, suggest an increasing institutionalization of these perspectives. A parallel growth has occurred in conflict management and dispute resolution as professions. And alternative (to the courts) dispute resolution has become a growth industry in the U.S.

THE ROLE OF CITIZEN INTERVENORS

The tradition of private citizen intervention has broadened in scope and deepened in conviction. It began as humble advice to government. Then it became the insistence on a citizen's right to be included "at the table." Subsequently it became massive intervention to alter the government's violence-producing policies. Finally, it has become a training and direct involvement initiative, officially acknowledged as part of global peacemaking.

Now, the citizen intervenor (CI) (to reduce violence) is one who: lobbies government on foreign policies such as arms sales; invests capital with informed social responsibility; trains in conflict moderation techniques; uses nonviolent action to thwart violence; and participates in domestic and transnational peace team missions.

How can we promote greater citizen intervention to confront violence? First, we can take advantage of a growing citizen inclination worldwide to challenge institutional policies and structures. Grassroots citizen action is indeed alive and very well. A global organizational infrastructure to promote intervention against violence and injustice might already be said to exist.

Second, we now have a substantial conflict knowledge pool available to the CI. The concepts and methods of conflict moderation are becoming simpler, are being translated into world languages and disseminated through citizen travel and electronic exchange: the emerging peacemaking discourse will touch people at all levels of society. An Internet conflict resolution course and exchange seminar we are developing at the University of Colorado (with U.S. Institute of Peace support) will help promote this initiative.

A growing pool of older persons in affluent nations now have the time, money, inclination and life experience to be trained and deployed as intervenors. And younger persons increasingly have families who will "stake" them in violence intervention missions. They may work in their home communities or alternate locales with transnational involvement. Organizations like Pangaea are responding to the increased demand for personal and peacemaker development.

DISCOURAGEMENTS

While others might call these initiatives wild dreaming, they stem instead from well-grounded speculation about the new possibilities for citizen intervention. Certainly, however, some global forces might discourage such initiatives. First, political, commercial and technological interests are now arming the world at a frightening rate: this may simply overwhelm nonmilitary intervention. The anti-personnel mine and the Pentagon's proposed arsenal ship, for example, are two diabolical, relatively cheap devices that further distance human perpetrators from the consequences of their violent acts, rendering them more difficult to deter.

Second, political and bureaucratic interests may resist private civilian intrusions into their preserve, even if ways were found to complement rather than complicate the crisis work of peacemaking professionals. To confront this resistance, citizen intervenors—among other things—would have to speak, at least minimally, the local language, and be sensitive to local peacemaking constraints.

Third, we neither fully understand nor can we fully predict the dynamics of external intervention. Neutrals intervening for humanitarian purposes may be regarded suspiciously in the "target" society, and may even be taken hostage. They may be ill-used by one side or another to demonstrate commitment or ruthlessness. Still, humanitarian organizations have accepted such risks for decades; their experience could continue to guide future citizen interventions. Ideally, organizational teams could be devised with coordinated in-country and intervening counterparts. City twinning, for example, might provide a structure for such violence reduction partnerships, not unlike the North Atlantic Treaty Organization's (NATO) logistical "forward positioning."

Most problematic would likely be the relationship of the CI to armed peacekeeping forces. If those forces were not perceived as completely neutral, civilian intervenors would also be tainted, as has occurred recently in Bosnia. Probably only by totally disconnecting the two will the CIs be viewed as neutral and nonthreatening. At the very least, their missions would have to be distinct, and a special relationship would have to be established to permit independent, effective interaction.

GREATER SUPPORT IS NEEDED

Despite the obstacles, countervailing conditions and institutions are now also providing greater support for direct citizen intervention in violence-ridden situations around the globe. They include expanding networks of conflict management, nonviolence and peace-building NGOs; a growing number of violence-attentive citizens; more research and teaching on violence reduction; and improved transnational electronic communications, permitting new forms of exchange and intervention.

The physical intervention of private citizens in high-risk areas of tension will likely increase only gradually. Both the would-be intervenors and the target societies must be protected. Rigorous training, apprenticeship and qualifying exams for such involvement may be necessary. Perhaps prior experience in violence reduction in one's own country should be a prerequisite for participation abroad.

MISSIONS AND GOALS

Besides preparation, we need clearly defined missions. A simple presence of intervenors, supporting themselves and doing things communities need done, might be one approach. The Shanti Sena, of the Gandhian movement in India, provides such a model. The brigadista coffee pickers in Nicaragua provide another.

Other energy sources for the citizen intervenor movement also exist. First, it can draw from the wealth of intervention experience accumulated by humanitarian organizations since World War II. Relief, development and human rights groups should be tapped for that knowledge.

Second, we should view citizen intervention as multidimensional. Working to humanize a government's land mine and firearms policies, for example, constitutes—even if indirectly—intervention for violence reduction in Bosnia, Cambodia, Angola, South Los Angeles, middle America, or in affluent Europe. Electronic communication can also help transnationalize such initiatives, promoting a kind of "intervention by idea." The modem is mightier than the sword. Peace and humanitarian organizations should learn from Amnesty International, which has refined citizen intervention with the pen, the cable and the computer. Current electronic advances should encourage the citizen activist to intervene everywhere.

Third, people could become more directly involved in group and national defense. The concepts of strategic nonviolence and nonmilitary defense have been evolving at least since 1960. Creating one's own defense rather than relying on armed protection by others may well be a citizen's most effective future security. In Western Europe, such thinking entered serious defense policy debates, notably in Germany, Scandinavia, and The Netherlands. Nonmilitary and non-provocative defense preparations may be important components of national and regional defense in the future.

THE BOSNIAN CIVIL WAR

With the "clarity of hindsight," how might citizen intervention have made a difference, for example, in moderating the Bosnian civil war? With more developed citizen intervention in place, this scenario might have evolved: European, North American and other governments having economic, political and military leverage in the former Yugoslavia, would have done everything possible to slow down the breakup process, beginning by refusing to immediately recognize the independence of the Yugoslav republics. Citizen intervenors would have counselled caution against precipitous actions.

Such intervention would have permitted time for: wiser decisions; government and civilian intervention networks to mobilize to protect at-risk minorities; resident observers to deter war crimes; community exchange programs and jointly run relief centers to allay interethnic hostility; developing interethnic solidarity networks across geographical ethnic lines; and training in non-military community defense.

The communication structure for this mobilization would have been partially in place through the earlier development of city-twinning programs, hot-response crisis management centers in the republics, and Internet peace action exchange groups. Yugoslav emigre volunteers from intervenor states might have been trained in multi-ethnic teams as negotiators, mediators, community organizers and other peacemaking roles.

By early 1992, a sufficient transnational and transrepublic civilian presence might have existed in Bosnia to weaken the pull of Croatian and Serbian nationalism, and their militarist proponents. That might well have permitted multi-ethnic Bosnian nationalism to withstand those centrifugal tendencies, as it very nearly did on its own.

The CIs of the future would be entrepreneurs. They would

mobilize resources—knowledge, motivation, and personal and organizational funds—to intervene for violence reduction at different levels and in diverse settings. A global set of interconnected networks is now emerging to promote that intervention. Citizen intervenors will be limited only by their personal availability, motivation, and imagination.

In the 21st century we will see private citizens, individually and collectively, assume a more important role, working beside state diplomats, humanitarian relief professionals and military peacekeepers, as a force against violence around the world. Citizen intervenors will intervene directly with their physical presence, and indirectly with their efforts to stem weapons proliferation and other policies that encourage state violence. With an exploding population straining its political, economic and natural resources, the future world will need to develop to the fullest its best potential for benign intervention.

"Gross violations of people's security justifie[s] intervention, and ... the principle of state sovereignty ... should not be allowed to bar international action on behalf of endangered people."

THE UNITED NATIONS SHOULD PROVIDE HUMANITARIAN INTERVENTION

Shridath Ramphal

The United Nations charter forbids intervention in the internal conflicts of nations unless they threaten international security. However, in the following viewpoint, Shridath Ramphal contends that when a nation's government threatens the security of its own people, other nations, working under the aegis of the United Nations, have a duty to intervene and restore the citizens' civil and human rights. The UN charter must be revised to permit these humanitarian interventions, the author maintains. Ramphal is the former secretary-general of the United Kingdom and the cochair of the Commission on Global Governance, an international organization devoted to improving social and economic conditions around the world.

As you read, consider the following questions:

1. In the author's opinion, why must the United Nations be the final arbiter of when humanitarian intervention is justified?
2. How are countries that intervene in another nation's domestic problems breaking the UN charter, according to Ramphal?
3. What two revisions to the UN Charter are recommended by the Commission on Global Governance, as cited by the author?

Excerpted from Shridath Ramphal, "Law and Intervention," *Peace Review*, vol. 8, no. 4 (December 1996), p. 493. Reprinted by permission.

In its international context, security has traditionally been defined as the security of states, the protection of their sovereignty and their physical integrity. Human society has, however, progressed to a stage where it is no longer comfortable with the exclusivity of that definition. It wants people to be brought within the concept of security. It feels that the world community should be concerned not only with the interests of states but also with the interests of people and their security.

We continue to live in a world of states, with an international system in which states are the dominant players. It is, however, a world in transition, one in which the rights of people are increasingly insistent, if not universally ascendant. Humanitarian intervention is a response to calls to recognize and protect those rights. It generally involves action against states that fail to respect them, based on the principle that the rights of people need to be upheld even, at times, against the rights of states.

The evolution of humanitarian issues to prominence on the world agenda is one of the most significant developments of the post-war period. The wider respect for human rights and the international arrangements developed to protect them reflect that progress. That humanitarian intervention has become more respectable is also evidence of that progress. But satisfaction on this score must be tempered, since willful human action endangering human security on a scale so substantial as to give rise to the need for intervention points not to progress but to retrogression.

WHEN INTERNATIONAL INTERVENTION IS JUSTIFIED

The question of intervention exercised the Commission on Global Governance a great deal. The principles of sovereignty and non-intervention have been bedrock concepts of the international legal order and we did not think they had outlived their validity. We were convinced, however, as we have said in our report *Our Global Neighborhood*, that "a global consensus exists today for a U.N. response on humanitarian grounds in cases of gross abuse of the security of people."

We were convinced that gross violations of people's security justified intervention, and that the principle of state sovereignty and the taboo against intervention in domestic affairs should not be allowed to bar international action on behalf of endangered people. We concluded that international law should expressly recognize the legitimacy of international intervention to put an end to such violations.

The line separating what should remain a matter of purely domestic jurisdiction from a situation in which international intervention is justified is a matter for considered judgment, but it is not difficult to sense when the violations have been so extensive that that line has been crossed. Few can dispute that it was crossed in Somalia, Rwanda, Bosnia, and earlier in places as various as apartheid South Africa, Khmer Rouge Cambodia and Amin's Uganda. Each situation, of course, has its own character and the response—the nature of intervention—must naturally be fashioned to suit its particular circumstances.

We were equally convinced, however, that judgments as to when such intervention is justified should be global decisions, made by the world community through its legitimate instrument, the United Nations (U.N.). It would be dangerous in the extreme to accept a general right of humanitarian intervention to be exercised by any state or states capable of doing so. That could pave the way for unilateral action, for vigilante action, for what one colleague described as intervention by the "sheriff's posse" on the international stage.

If the principle of non-intervention is to be set aside in exceptional circumstances, it must be done by the community of states acting democratically. States should not have the right to use force unilaterally, save in their own defense. That principle needs to be preserved, or the weak would be at the mercy of the strong and the predatory. Beyond self-defense, the use of force against countries should be under the authority and control of the U.N. on behalf of the global community. That must be a norm of global security. We must guard against intervention determined by the interests of particular countries, countries that are powerful globally or within a region. It could be all too easy to intervene in the name of protecting the security of people— aggression, invasion, military intrusion, masquerading as international virtue. Any regime of humanitarian intervention must therefore be rigorously patrolled by the rule of international law.

THE U.N. CHARTER

The U.N. Charter forbids intervention in matters of domestic jurisdiction, countenancing intervention only in situations that are a threat to international peace and security. In these circumstances the U.N. has so far been able to authorize interventions in response to humanitarian tragedies within countries only by bending the provisions of the Charter, subjecting them to what has been called "creative interpretation." "Hard cases make bad law" is as true globally as nationally. A Charter that bends to power cannot stand for the rule of law. It is immensely preferable to change the Charter so that the U.N. is given the legal right to authorize intervention on humanitarian grounds when grave violations of people's security are perpetrated—even if they do not pose a threat to international peace and security. Only by changing the Charter can a "right" of intervention be effectively circumscribed.

The Charter should be revised to serve two objectives. One is to provide legal authority for humanitarian intervention. The other is to define the circumstances under which intervention may be authorized. The Charter amendment should therefore both license and limit intervention. Both functions are equally necessary. The authority to intervene, desirable as it is, should be exercised only in extreme circumstances. A Charter-based legal framework for international intervention would increase the prospect that intervention conforms to agreed criteria, is not arbitrary, and is reasonably consistent. It is a better, surer, way of securing sovereignty and freedom from intervention in all normal cases than allowing these principles to be qualified selectively on a basis of "creative ambiguity."

Two Examples

Two examples from the 1990s underline the dangers that can arise under the present unsatisfactory arrangements. Operation Provide Comfort was undertaken by a small group of states towards the end of the Gulf War. It was an act of military intervention in a domestic situation. It was contrary to the Charter of the U.N.; it was illegal, but because it was carried out at a time of such widespread revulsion against Iraqi treatment of the Kurdish people it was allowed without major international questioning. It is also arguable that it was less designed to provide comfort to the Kurdish people in Iraq than to make life more comfortable for the governments taking action—in the context of popular pressure within their own countries.

Haiti is my second example. The U.S. intervention in Haiti, authorized by the U.N., was palpably not undertaken because there was a threat to international peace and security. The U.S.'s Ambassador at the U.N., Madeleine Albright, openly described it as action to restore democracy. However respectable, even laudable, that objective may be, it is not one that international law in the form of the Charter recognizes as justifying external intervention. Again, there is room to question if the stated objective was the real objective. Was the primary objective to reinstate President Aristide in Port-au-Prince or to stem the tide of boat people heading for the shores of Florida trailing political embarrassment for the Clinton Administration?

Democracy has been suppressed elsewhere, sometimes as egregiously as in Haiti. In both Burma and Nigeria the will of the people expressed in democratic elections has been brutally defied. But there has been no international intervention to restore democracy in either country. It would seem that refugees from these countries must land on the shores of a Permanent Member of the Security Council, causing a domestic problem for its government, before any meaningful action by way of international intervention is contemplated.

Both operations, in Iraq and Haiti, demonstrate that at present there is a risk that intervention could be arbitrary and heavily influenced by the national interests of major powers rather than the humanitarian objectives of the world community. It is possible to think of other scenarios of the Security Council deciding, under pressure from powerful members acting in their own national interests, to intervene in a country where there are human rights abuses or a denial of democratic rights—but without the security of its people being extensively violated. These dangers support the case for establishing a clearer legal basis for international humanitarian intervention and defining the circumstances which would justify such action, so that there is respect for accepted principles, clearer criteria and greater consistency.

THE CHARTER MUST BE AMENDED

The view taken in the Commission on Global Governance is that if the Security Council is to disregard the prohibition against intervention in internal affairs written into Article 2.7 of the Charter, it should do so only in circumstances expressly laid down in the Charter and not by stretching the rules or interpreting them "creatively." We have proposed that the Charter should be amended by the introduction of a provision permitting such intervention but restricting it to situations in which the violation of the security of people is so gross and extreme as to require—in the judgment of a reformed Security Council—international intervention on humanitarian grounds. The Council would need to determine in each case whether, given the importance of the principles of sovereignty and non-interference in domestic affairs, the situation in a country had deteriorated to the point where the security of its people had been violated to a degree warranting international action. An affirmative conclusion by the Council would clear the way for U.N. action, duly authorized by the Council and carried out under its control on behalf of the world community.

An explicit provision in the Charter of the U.N. on these lines would signal the message that states can no longer count on the principles of sovereignty and non-intervention as legal shields if they flagrantly abuse the security of their people. The threat that state behavior of a certain kind could trigger an interdictory reaction from the world body can be expected to exercise some deterrence and thereby reduce the occasions when it is necessary to intervene.

AN OBLIGATION TO GLOBAL HUMANITY

Should we put soldiers at risk in faraway places when our own country is not under attack or threatened with attack (not Maine or Georgia or Oregon) and when national interests, narrowly understood, are not at stake? I am strongly inclined, sometimes, to give a positive answer to this question (whether volunteers or conscripts should bear these risks is too complicated to take up here). The reason is simple enough: all states have an interest in global stability and even in global humanity, and in the case of wealthy and powerful states like ours, this interest is seconded by obligation. No doubt, the "civilized" world is capable of living with grossly uncivilized behavior in places like East Timor, say—offstage and out of sight. But behavior of that kind, unchallenged, tends to spread, to be imitated or reiterated. Pay the moral price of silence and callousness, and you will soon have to pay the political price of turmoil and lawlessness nearer home.

Michael Walzer, *Dissent*, Winter 1995.

To give the Security Council express authority under the Charter to intervene in certain circumstances will not, of course, guarantee that it does intervene. A Charter amendment placing intervention on a sounder legal footing may make the Council readier to take action but cannot compel it to do so. The Council consists of a number of governments, with a membership subject to a degree of periodic change. It will make up its mind on each case and it may, for various reasons, be more exercised over some situations than others. That there is a tendency among governments not to rush to place other governments in the dock on "domestic" issues is also a fact that has to be recognized.

LEGITIMACY AND CONSISTENCY

It is desirable, therefore, not only that international intervention should have legitimacy but also that there should both be a high degree of consistency in the reactions of the world community to grave violations of people's security and a high degree of probability that such transgressions would not be ignored or tolerated.

It is also desirable that the world body, besides being ready to intervene when extensive violations of people's security have occurred, should also take action to deter and prevent such violations where there is advance knowledge of the possibility of their taking place. These considerations led the Commission on Global Governance to propose the establishment of machinery to enable civil society to alert governments and urge them to consider action by bringing before the U.N. situations in which the security of people is or could be extensively endangered.

The proposal is for a Council for Petitions to be created within the U.N. to whose attention civil society organizations would have the right to bring situations within countries which in their view threatened to endanger the lives of people on a large scale. It is not envisaged that the Council itself would have the power to intervene but it would have the authority to make recommendations and call for action by the appropriate U.N. body, including the Security Council. . . .

This proposal recognizes the enhanced role of civil society organizations in articulating and protecting the interests of people. Many of them have acquired a capacity to contribute to humanitarian relief efforts. What is even more pertinent to the present discussion is that there are non-governmental organizations that are able, because of their involvement at the grassroots, to spot signs of growing tension and provide early warning of impending crises. Some NGOs have attributes that enable them to help in efforts to prevent and resolve conflicts. The Council would provide such bodies a formal channel of access to the global intergovernmental forum of the U.N. on matters vital to the security—and survival—of people. It would offer them means to prod governments to take note of "domestic" situations in which the security of people may be placed at risk and which therefore merit the attention of the world community.

"The real purpose of 'humanitarian' intervention . . . is . . . to bolster the existing class structure, . . . while keeping the whole repressive system intact."

HUMANITARIAN INTERVENTION IS SOMETIMES HARMFUL

Michael Parenti

The United States has an ulterior motive in providing humanitarian intervention to nations in crisis, argues Michael Parenti in the following viewpoint. He contends that the United States intervenes in a nation's domestic affairs only when it needs to protect American business interests and create opportunities for new investments. Such interventions do little to help the countries' oppressed citizens, he asserts, but do much to help their oppressors. Parenti is the author of several books including *Democracy for the Few* and *Land of Idols: Political Mythology in America*.

As you read, consider the following questions:

1. According to Parenti, how did the U.S. intervention in Haiti help foreign investors and harm the country's poor?
2. What was the real purpose of U.S. intervention in Haiti, in the author's opinion?
3. What is a necessary condition for a successful intervention, in Parenti's view?

Reprinted from Michael Parenti, "Myths of 'Humanitarian' Intervention," *Against the Current*, November/December 1995, by permission of *Against the Current*.

C ontrary to popular belief, U.S. leaders are no different from those of most other countries in that they have a dismal humanitarian record.

True, many nations including this one have sent relief abroad in response to particular disasters. But these sporadic actions are limited in scope, do not represent an essential policy commitment, and obscure the many occasions when governments choose to do absolutely nothing for other peoples in dire straits.

In addition, most U.S. aid missions serve as pretexts for hidden political agendas. They are intended to bolster conservative pro-capitalist regimes, build infrastructures (roads, ports, office complexes) that assist big investors, lend a cover for counterinsurgency programs, and undermine local agrarian self-sufficiency by driving independent farmers off lands that are then taken over by corporate agribusiness.

Be it the indigenous rain forest peoples of South America and Southeast Asia, or the Kurds, Biafrans or Palestinians; be it the overseas Chinese in Indonesia, or the East Timorese, Cambodians, Angolans, Mozambicans, Guatemalans, Salvadorans or dozens of other peoples, U.S. rulers have done little to help rescue them from their terrible plights, and in most instances have done much to assist their oppressors.

CASE STUDY: HAITI

Consider the "good intervention" in Haiti. For over three years of military rule, while some 10,000 political murders took place, Washington did nothing to restore democracy in that country. The CIA issued a report claiming that the deposed president, Jean-Bertrand Aristide, was mentally unbalanced.

In 1990, the left-populist Aristide had won an overwhelming 70 percent of the vote, much to the dismay of the U.S. State Department and White House.

In September, 1994, the White House invaded and occupied Haiti with the professed intent of reviving democracy and reinstating Aristide. But the restoration was to come at a heavy price.

Aristide was strongarmed into accepting a World Bank agreement that included (a) shifting some presidential powers to the conservative Haitian parliament, (b) massive privatization of the public sector, (c) a 50 percent cut in public employment, (d) a reduction in regulation and taxes on U.S. companies investing in Haiti, (e) increased subsidies for exports and private corporations, and (f) a lowering of import duties.

In addition, Aristide was made to drop his land reform and social security programs and any plans to boost the minimum wage from $2 to $4 a day (not an hour). World Bank representatives admitted that all these measures would hurt the Haitian poor but benefit the "enlightened business investors."

Former national security advisor James Schlesinger (ABC-TV, September 16, 1994) noted that U.S. forces were needed to prevent "the Aristide people from making reprisals." Many of them are poor, he said, and may want to loot the houses of the rich.

INTERVENTION CAN WORSEN THE SITUATION

To intervene out of humanitarian concern without any idea of what comes next often does as much to worsen the situation in the long run as it does to alleviate things in the short term.

In Somalia, where the United States became involved to a large extent because of pressure from groups like CARE, we learned how quickly humanitarian interventions can go awry.

David Rieff, *New York Times*, November 14, 1996.

Indeed, U.S. troops were deployed to protect upscale neighborhoods. Meanwhile, U.S. military intelligence worked closely with Haitian intelligence, and the United States prepared to bolster existing police and military forces with special training programs—over the protests of the Aristide government.

During the occupation, U.S. firms in Haiti have continued to fire people who try to unionize, while paying workers ten to twenty cents an hour for a ten-hour day. Meanwhile conditions go from bad to worse: According to the World Bank itself, the number of Haitians who live in absolute destitution rose from 48 percent in 1976 to 81 percent in 1985, ushering in serious spread of disease and malnutrition.

LEARNING THE LESSONS

While ballyhooed by the White House and the media as a rescue operation for democracy, the real purpose of "humanitarian" intervention in Haiti is no different from interventions in numerous other countries: to bolster the existing class structure, enhance the prerogatives of large investors, suppress or otherwise disempower popular organizations and their leaders, and engage in a mild facelift of the military and police by easing out some of the more notorious repressors while keeping the whole repressive system intact.

In 1915, the last time U.S. troops purified Haiti, they killed 15,000 Haitians and did not depart until 1934—and then only after setting up an autocratic military apparatus that has remained more or less in place to this day, propped up by U.S. military force.

A number of countries have endured this process of having a reformist government subjected to U.S.-sponsored destabilization, the economy forced into a still more stringent colonization and the shell of democracy maintained or reintroduced after a period of covert violence or overt military repression.

One can think of Greece, Jamaica, the Dominican Republic, Nicaragua, Chile and other nations as instances where political democracy is allowed to survive only if it is not used to initiate a genuine economic democracy.

PROTECTING FOREIGN INVESTMENTS

In sum, the function of U.S. intervention is to protect U.S. investments in other countries and create opportunities for new investments. Even more important is the general commitment to safeguarding the global class system and its free-market capital accumulation process.

Irrespective of the amount of direct investment held by U.S. firms in any particular country, the overriding imperative is to keep the world's land, labor, natural resources and markets accessible to transnational investors on the most favorable possible terms.

To carry out these functions it is necessary to suppress popular governments and movements—and even, as in Iraq, conservative military ones—that are economically nationalistic.

U.S. leaders find it necessary to convince the U.S. public that such things are being done for our benefit and security and in order to make the world a better place for all. The empire can survive only by expropriating the resources of the Republic. Thus a compliant public, willing to shoulder the immense costs of a globally repressive apparatus, is a necessary condition for intervention.

The left's task is to show U.S. citizens how their interests are being regularly violated, how they carry the costs of empire (exportation of jobs, high taxes, loss of loved ones in the military, impoverishment of domestic services), and how it is in their best interests and the interests of peoples abroad to oppose the aggressions of the U.S. national security state.

THE "NEW WORLD ORDER"

Call it the "New World Order," the "post–Cold War period," the "era of economic globalization" or whatever. Imperialism is the real name of the game. And while some of the tactics may change over time, the game itself remains essentially the same.

| "Humanitarian action is noble when coupled with political action and justice. Without them, it is doomed to failure and . . . becomes little more than a plaything of international politics."

HUMANITARIAN INTERVENTION MUST BE TIED TO POLITICAL CHANGE

Alain Destexhe

Alain Destexhe is secretary general of Médecins sans Frontières (Doctors Without Borders), an international organization that provides medical care to people in danger due to war, epidemics, or natural disasters. In the following viewpoint, Destexhe contends that the United Nations has changed its mission from one of peacekeeping to one of providing humanitarian aid to refugees in war-torn areas. This new "emergency ethic" of supplying food and shelter to the victims of war serves only to salve the conscience of the international community and does little to change their plight, he maintains. He argues that while providing humanitarian aid to warring countries is a moral obligation, it will not prevent future genocide unless the conditions that led to the war are changed and justice is provided to the persecuted.

As you read, consider the following questions:

1. What were the adverse effects of the humanitarian aid sent to Rwanda, according to Destexhe?
2. What is the greatest threat to the international society, in the author's opinion?

Reprinted from Alain Destexhe, "Stopping Bloodshed," OneWorld, March 1995, by permission of the World Council of Churches.

T he construction of a new world order and the development of the United Nations organisation since the Second World War have been guided by the principle: Never Again.

The Nazis' unprecedented crime against the Jews became a benchmark for an international community founded on certain basic values: opposition to genocide, the search for world peace and respect for human rights.

THE TUTSI MASSACRE

Now, only 50 years later, the world has failed to react to the first indisputable genocide since that perpetrated against the Jews. It has stood back and allowed between half a million and a million people in Rwanda to be massacred with impunity simply because they were born Tutsis.

The victims of the massacres that began 6 April 1994 initially included both Hutus and Tutsis. There was, however, one fundamental difference. Whereas Hutus belonging to the democratic opposition or to human rights organisations were murdered for their political convictions, Tutsis were slaughtered simply for being Tutsis.

A genocide is an exceptional event in 20th-century history. The term was first used in 1944 to qualify the massive crimes against humanity committed by the Nazis in occupied Europe. Since then the word genocide has so often been misused in attempts to capture attention by drawing parallels with the crime of the century that it has become synonymous with any act of mass murder.

And yet genocide is defined not by the number of victims or the cruelty of the act, but solely by the deliberate intention to exterminate a national, ethnic, racial or religious group. The crime is characterised by the targeting of a specific group for no other reason than its very existence. As the etymology suggests, the term does not apply to politically defined groups, but exclusively to those constituted by race, ethnicity, nationality or religion.

INDIFFERENCE TO GENOCIDE

The simple fact that it was possible, in 1944, to commit genocide amid widespread indifference raises grave questions about the constraints placed by the world on the instigators and perpetrators of mass murder.

First, what does "international community" mean? This vague notion of belonging to a community of nations, entailing rights, responsibilities and rules of conduct, has been evolving since the 16th century. It began to pick up speed with the setting up of the League of Nations, acquiring still greater momentum after 1945 through the United Nations (UN).

As the end of the twentieth century nears, this community might reasonably be expected at least to protect its members when they find themselves the target of radical extermination attempts. This did not happen in Rwanda.

Second, the UN, and above all the major powers involved, placed the instigators of genocide and the Rwandan Patriotic Front on the same footing: once again they delayed before taking sides, and once again their intervention—after between half a million and a million people had died—came in the form of humanitarian aid for the Hutu refugees, the Tutsis inside Rwanda having been almost entirely wiped out.

MORE THAN HUMANITARIAN AID IS NEEDED

There is no such thing as a purely humanitarian intervention; any and all must be undertaken with realistic political goals—there is no point, for example, in setting up new refugee camps if they are again to become incubators of terror and death. The [local militias] must be separated from the general population to prevent relief supplies from feeding a new disaster. . . . We will have been compassionate, but in the end we will have guaranteed another crisis.

Michael Maren, *Nation*, December 9, 1996.

Humanitarian action is playing an increasingly ambiguous role in international crises. While one can only rejoice at the massive sympathy inspired throughout the world by the human catastrophe of the Hutu exodus, itself organised by the genocide's perpetrators, this wave of human feeling came when the genocide had been accomplished.

This praiseworthy mobilisation was not, however, without side-effects. It pushed the genocide into the background, wiping away the shame of the initial failure to act and giving the world something to feel good about. It is increasingly becoming a feature of modern society that anything goes as long as a few fire-fighters are allowed to fling the occasional bucket of relief at the political house fire.

Finally, justice may well become a political imperative. It is necessary not only for the victims, but also for international order. Not to judge the perpetrators and instigators of the genocide would be not only a terrible injustice but a grave political error.

There is enormous potential in the world today for crises

with an ethnic dimension to take place. The greatest threat to society internationally is the rebirth of racist ideologies, with their racial hierarchies that reject and exclude all others. From Burma to Sudan, the Caucasus to the former Yugoslavia, Bosnia and Zaire, such racism is flourishing. If the international community allows these ideologies to provoke genocide, relief organisations will be left helpless.

Hot on the heels of Bosnia and Somalia, the Rwandan crisis bears out the major trend discernible in the management of international crises. The honeymoon period, that began with the end of the cold war and the dreams of a new world order, seems to be over.

The major powers have made it clear that the UN is not going to be the world's police officer, and that none of them is able or willing to take on the job. After a period of rapid expansion, peace-keeping operations have come to a halt.

The Rwanda situation was the first time that the international organisation responded to a crisis not by stepping up its involvement but by a brutal disengagement, cutting the UN Assistance Mission to Rwanda (UNAMIR) forces from 2,500 to 270.

In the former Yugoslavia, Médecins sans Frontières has repeatedly attacked the strictly humanitarian approach prevalent since the conflict started. Coming after Srebrenica and Gorazde, the siege of Bihac was just a further illustration of the powerlessness of the UN—and now of the North Atlantic Treaty Organization (NATO).

There has been repeated talk of withdrawing the peace-keeping forces. Yet aid to the victims is not negotiable: it is a moral obligation quite independent of the success of any political settlement. The subsequent failure of any such settlement would not be a valid excuse for the UN and the European Union to abandon or reduce their relief efforts, which must continue regardless of the political situation, as long as people are suffering.

The European Union has for a long time limited its involvement to relief work. Were it to stop or reduce its aid on the pretext that the parties had failed to reach agreement, it would only underline the hypocrisy and cynicism of its earlier policy.

FAILED HUMANITARIAN AID

All over the world, there is unprecedented enthusiasm for humanitarian work. It is far from certain that this is always in the victims' best interests. Considerable progress was made at the end of the 1970s, when there was at last an end to the judgment of victims from an ideological perspective. The dead were no longer good or bad, but victims deserving of compassion.

This new perspective gave rise to an "emergency ethic", which has become increasingly prevalent. However, we were quick to forget that the western values during the cold war were combined with *Realpolitik* to counter totalitarian thinking.

Nowadays, from Bosnia to Rwanda, the emergency ethic has rebounded on the victims. They are now seen in terms of their immediate suffering rather than as fellow human beings, hungry mouths to feed rather than citizens fighting for values or simply to stay alive.

Humanitarian aid was Europe's only real response to Serb aggression in Bosnia. This same response was proffered in Rwanda, when the genocide was over and it was too late. Here the massive deployment of humanitarian aid around Goma somehow disguised the culpable failure to come to the assistance of Tutsis in mortal danger.

In Bosnia, humanitarian aid elevated to the status of official policy has, in the final analysis, encouraged and fostered aggression while bringing public opinion to accept both the *fait accompli* of the stronger party and an "ethnic" reading of the conflict.

The humanitarian brotherhood is playing an increasingly amnesic role, preventing all political analysis of the situation, sustaining the impression that these supposedly tribal struggles defy comprehension.

In dealing with countries in ongoing wars of a local nature, humanitarian aid has acquired a near-monopoly of morality and international action. It is this monopoly that we seek to denounce.

POLITICAL ACTION IS NECESSARY

Humanitarian action is noble when coupled with political action and justice. Without them, it is doomed to failure and, especially in the major crises covered by the media, becomes little more than a plaything of international politics, a conscience-salving gimmick.

There is an enormous disparity today between the principles and values proclaimed by our societies on the one hand, and the measures taken to defend them on the other.

We now endlessly commemorate past struggles against tyranny, congratulate ourselves on the mythical advance of justice and, at the same time, stand by idly when faced with the first indisputable genocide since the Second World War or the return of "ethnic cleansing" to the heart of Europe.

How can we think of passing food through the window while doing nothing to drive the murderer from the house, feeding hostages without attempting to confront their kidnapper, or, worse still, feeding the murderer after the crime?

These are not humanitarian acts. Nevertheless, a purely humanitarian approach acts as a blindfold which allows us to bask permanently in the warmth of our own generosity. A perverse concept of humanitarian action may well triumph in the absence of policy and justice. It is far from certain that the victims are getting anything out of it.

PERIODICAL BIBLIOGRAPHY

The following articles have been selected to supplement the diverse views presented in this chapter. Addresses are provided for periodicals not indexed in the *Readers' Guide to Periodical Literature*, the *Alternative Press Index*, the *Social Sciences Index*, or the *Index to Legal Periodicals and Books*.

Gail Chaddock and Judith Matloff	"West Split on Sending Troops to Zaire," *Christian Science Monitor*, November 12, 1996.
Christopher M. Gray	"Humanitarian Intervention," *Current*, February 1998.
Chris Hedges	"Despite U.N. Role, Serbs Find No Peace in Croatia," *New York Times*, March 19, 1998.
Issues and Controversies On File	"U.S. Intervention in Africa," August 8, 1997. Available from Facts On File, 11 Penn Plaza, New York, NY 10001-2006.
Michael Maren	"Feeding Africa's Crises," *Nation*, December 9, 1996.
Anne McCarthy	"Why Is Nonviolence So Threatening?" *Salt of the Earth*, January/February 1995. Available from 205 W. Monroe St., Chicago, IL 60606.
Andrew S. Natsios	"Hutus, Tutsis, and Us," *Weekly Standard*, December 16, 1996. Available from 1211 Avenue of the Americas, New York, NY 10036.
New York Times	"A Useful Balkan Firewall," March 2, 1998.
Michael E. O'Hanlon	"A Debate About the Future of Bosnia: Turning the Bosnia Ceasefire into Peace," *Brookings Review*, Winter 1998.
William J. Perry and Warren Christopher	"NATO's Next Mission," *Hoover Digest*, Spring 1998. Available from Hoover Press, Stanford University, Stanford, CA 94305-6010.
David Rieff	"Realpolitik in Congo," *Nation*, July 7, 1997.
David Rieff and Brian Urquhart	"Saving the World: The Limits of Humanitarianism," *Nation*, May 19, 1997.
Deborah Tannen	"Managing Confrontations: Lessons from Abroad," *Responsive Community*, Spring 1998. Available from 2020 Pennsylvania Ave. NW, #282, Washington, DC 20006-1846.

CHAPTER 3

WHAT ROLE SHOULD THE U.S. PLAY IN MAINTAINING PEACE?

CHAPTER PREFACE

Some foreign policy experts argue that since communism is no longer a global threat, the United States should give up its role as a world peacekeeper and concentrate on domestic policies. Solving the world's conflicts is a role better suited to the United Nations, they contend. By transferring this responsibility to the UN, these analysts maintain that the United States can focus on resolving its domestic problems. Funds that were once slated for foreign aid and defense can now be used to improve education, develop inner cities, reduce taxes, and rebuild the economy.

Other foreign policy analysts contend, however, that the United States cannot afford to ignore the world's problems. They warn that isolationism by the United States could lead to political instability around the world. Nations that could no longer depend on the United States for protection would feel the need to rearm themselves, which could lead to heightened tensions and the possibility of war. Furthermore, these experts maintain that the threat of U.S. intervention is enough to prevent tyranny and oppression in many countries. If the United States refuses to protect democracy around the world, despotic regimes that may arise could eventually threaten the United States. Former president Ronald Reagan declared in 1986, "Our own freedom, and that of our allies, could never be secure in a world where freedom was threatened everywhere else."

Whether the United States should intervene in foreign wars and what kind of intervention is effective in ending these conflicts are among the issues examined by the authors in the following chapter.

> "[The United States is] the only big kid on the block, and history has brought us to a place where the main global business at hand is to deal with these small, ugly world conflicts."

THE UNITED STATES SHOULD INTERVENE IN REGIONAL CONFLICTS

Andrew Bard Schmookler

The United States, as the last of the superpowers, has the duty and moral obligation to send its military forces to the world's trouble spots, argues Andrew Bard Schmookler in the following viewpoint. He contends that unless the United States contributes to these humanitarian or peacekeeping missions, other nations will be reluctant to participate, which will result in a massive human catastrophe. Furthermore, Schmookler maintains, it is in the country's best interests to use its power to help those in need. Schmookler is a columnist and the author of several books on war and values.

As you read, consider the following questions:

1. Why should the lives of American soldiers be put at risk in global conflicts when American interests are not at stake, according to Schmookler?
2. In the author's opinion, why is it senseless for the world to stand back and let a besieged people work out their problems for themselves?
3. According to Schmookler, how does U.S. intervention in foreign countries differ from the U.S. welfare system?

Reprinted from Andrew Bard Schmookler, "The Willingness to Help," *The Christian Science Monitor*, Opinion/Essays, December 23, 1996, by permission of the author.

When the United States was on the verge of sending troops to Zaire to help prevent people from starving, we started hearing the usual complaints. Not our business. Not a drop of American blood. Not the right use for American forces.

There's something unseemly about these arguments.

ISOLATIONISM

It has often been noted that some of the same people who were dovish during the old cold-war days—when the US was struggling for its survival—are the first to want to send in the Marines for humanitarian reasons, when our vital national interests are not clearly at stake. But what troubles me is the other side of that picture, the way some of the old hawks are eager to prevent American troops from taking even the slightest risk when "all" that is to be gained is the preservation of innumerable human lives and of some last vestiges of civilized values.

The arguments advanced for this isolationist position seem flawed. If you listened to the case against using US troops in a place like Zaire, you'd never know Americans were going to be a small part of a larger international effort. The opponents ask, "Why should American boys take risks where American interests are not at stake?" They never ask, "Why should we join with the rest of the civilized world in saving many lives with limited risk to ourselves?" The mission in Zaire was to be led by the Canadians, but to listen to the critics on the television commentary circuit you'd think it was just us Yanks being dragged into something that was none of our affair.

These critics don't want the US to be 911 to the world, but they never say who should be 911 to people being starved and terrorized in Africa, or raped and bombarded in Bosnia. I'd feel better about their concerns if the same people who say American troops should only be used to protect American interests were also pressing to have an international force established that could fill this need.

AVERTING CATASTROPHE

Make no mistake: In these situations, if nothing is done by outsiders with no vital interests at stake, the result will be human catastrophe. It makes no sense to talk about leaving a problem to "the Haitian people" to resolve, when a group of thugs has seized power and has the population terrorized. The exodus of refugees back to Rwanda as soon as the genocidal clique holding them captive had been run off shows that it was precisely the wider world's unwillingness to provide but the tiniest show of force . . . that allowed that crisis to develop. And it was only when the North Atlantic Treaty Organization (NATO) at last ran a few bombing missions over Bosnia in 1995 that the bloodshed there came to an end.

With just a little effort in these situations we can bring a kind of peace and justice to places where the most brutal kind of might otherwise substitutes for right. But the opponents say no, it's not our affair. Many of these are the same people who insist on beefing up the Pentagon's budget, even beyond what the Joint Chiefs want. Yet what do they want us to do with this immense force when there is no one else remotely in our league? We're spending almost as much on defense as the rest of the world combined. Are we being prepared for a worst-case scenario of America versus the world? We're the only big kid on the block, and history has brought us to a place where the main global business at hand is to deal with these small, ugly world conflicts.

1995 DEFENSE SPENDING IN BILLIONS OF U.S. DOLLARS

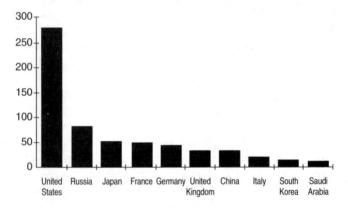

International Institute for Strategic Studies, *The Military Balance 1996–1997*, 1996.

For the first time in history, "little" nightmares such as these—where the fate of "only" a few million people at a time hangs in the balance—can be ended by a coherent world, one with eyes to see into the world's dark and distant crevices, and the forums in which to decide together that humankind stands for more than brutal force and selfish indifference.

EVEN IN SOMALIA

Even in Somalia, more than a dozen Americans died, but hundreds of thousands of people who would have died survived because of us. Is it not part of our national interest to know and to show that this is what America is—not just a power bent on its own gain but a nation consecrated to doing God's work?

A comparison with the welfare debate comes to mind. I used to think that conservatives who resented the welfare system were simply selfish—that they'd rather have the money in their own comparatively well-lined pockets than to have to give up some so that the poorest among us had food and shelter.

But I've come since to learn that in many cases I was wrong. Some of these conservatives were right that the welfare system perpetuated many of the same problems it was supposed to solve. They were right that the huge paternalistic bureaucracies of government were less effective in changing lives than the private giving that some churches and community groups practice. And I saw that many who didn't want their taxes going into a welfare state were generous in funding these other ways of being a good Samaritan.

OUR CHOICES

But in places such as Zaire and Bosnia there is no private way of changing lives. In such situations there is no "culture of dependency" that degrades people who might otherwise rely upon themselves. It is a choice between putting ourselves out for our wounded neighbor by the side of the road or just letting him bleed to death. It is a choice between using the tool of official armed forces, or letting the most monstrous of our kind define the face of our times. To refuse to extend ourselves in situations like that seems to me just plain selfishness of the kind that all our values, all our spiritual traditions, tell us not to indulge in. We're better than that, aren't we?

"We are inviting a day when our
enemies, seeing that we cannot
conceivably cover all our IOUs, are
going to make a concerted run on
the bank."

THE UNITED STATES SHOULD NOT
INTERVENE IN REGIONAL CONFLICTS

Patrick J. Buchanan

In the following viewpoint, Patrick J. Buchanan argues that the
United States should not intervene in regional conflicts where the
nation has no vital interests that need protecting, such as in
Bosnia. The Europeans are fully capable of defending themselves,
Buchanan asserts, and they should finally own up to their responsibility. Buchanan argues that America's overseas defense commitments have stretched the U.S. military to the point that the
United States would be unable to defend itself against a concerted
attack by its enemies. U.S. forces should be removed immediately
from overseas, Buchanan insists. Buchanan, a senior adviser to
Richard Nixon, Gerald Ford, and Ronald Reagan, ran for the Republican presidential nomination in 1992 and 1996. He is a syndicated columnist and the author of *The Great Betrayal: How American
Sovereignty and Social Justice Are Sacrificed to the Gods of the Global Economy.*

As you read, consider the following questions:

1. How does Buchanan respond to the argument that NATO will
   collapse if the United States withdraws from Europe?
2. What countries other than Bosnia has the United States made
   a commitment to defend, according to the author?
3. How does Buchanan respond to the charge that he and his
   colleagues are isolationists?

H is mentors at Georgetown and Oxford would be proud.
For Bill Clinton emerged as the true heir of Woodrow Wilson. In the name of "democracy" and "peace," he committed the U.S. Army to a blood-soaked Balkan peninsula where no vital U.S. interest is at risk—to advance his vision of a new world order.

Whatever may be said of him, Clinton put his presidency on the line, boldly. And our Republican Congress?

Newt Gingrich and Bob Dole, like umpires in a college debate, urge that the President be given a chance to make his case for going in.

But what do they themselves believe? Well, they have doubts, but are open to persuasion.

There are several ways to characterize the Republican posture. Leadership, however, is not one of them.

A Permanent Military Presence

History will look back on this Bosnian adventure as a turning point. With the Cold War over, the Soviet empire dissolved, the United States decided on a permanent military presence in Europe, accepting prime responsibility, in perpetuity, for Europe's security and peace.

No referendum was ever held on this momentous decision.

Why are we doing it? Because we are admonished; If we do not, U.S. global leadership is gone and NATO itself will perish. But does anyone believe that Europeans, free riders for 50 years on U.S. defense, will inform us that we may no longer protect them, if we do not put 20,000 troops into Bosnia?

This Bosnian crisis is the time to tell the Europeans what they should have been told years ago: Defense of their continent is now their responsibility. Why must 260 million Americans defend forever 300 million Europeans from 160 million Russians mired in poverty and despair? How long must their damnable dependency endure?

Our foreign policy Establishment is behaving with all the hubris of The Best and The Brightest who marched us into Vietnam. Under interventionists of both parties, U.S. foreign policy is being driven headlong toward bankruptcy.

Strategic liabilities—commitments to go to war to defend other nations—are annually expanded, as the assets to cover those liabilities—U.S. military power are drawn down. Since the Gulf War, U.S. armed forces have mustered out the equal of the entire Army of Desert Storm.

Yet consider our recent war guarantees: We are committed to

defend Kuwait, to "dual containment" of Iran and Iraq, to protect Iraq's Shiites and Kurds. We have put 2,000 troops in Haiti, 500 in Macedonia, as a trip wire to involve us in any war that erupts in the Southern Balkans and have pledged troops for the Golan Heights.

Clinton is sending 20,000 into Bosnia.

Among the NATO "expansionists," moderates want war guarantees given to Poland, Hungary, Slovakia, the Czech Republic; the militants want war guarantees given to Lithuania, Latvia, Estonia, Ukraine. Should Russian nationalist Alexander Lebed become president and seek to reassert Moscow's influence, a U.S.-Russia collision would be certain. To enhance its probability, we have approved introduction of Russian combat troops, alongside Serbs, in Bosnia. Add our old Cold War commitments to defend 15 NATO allies, Japan, Korea, Australia, New Zealand, the Southeast Asia Treaty Organization (SEATO) nations and Israel, and we have virtually ensured that no major war can break out, anywhere, without U.S. involvement, from Day One.

This is not statesmanship; It is imperial overstretch. We are inviting a day when our enemies, seeing that we cannot conceivably cover all our IOUs, are going to make a concerted run on the bank.

NOTHING TO DO WITH AMERICA

The efforts of Serbia to retain its own territory is none of the North Atlantic Treaty Organization's business. It's not our business either. . . .

We have a full domestic agenda, and neither money nor lives should be wasted on faraway foreign quarrels and intrigues. God did not anoint the United States to govern the world. The United States is not competent to govern the world. The Constitution does not authorize the United States government to govern the world. The American people don't want to govern the world.

Charley Reese, *Conservative Chronicle*, June 24, 1998.

After our Cold War triumph, some of us pleaded for a complete review of all extraordinary Cold War commitments and a return to a traditional foreign policy rooted in U.S. national interests.

For this we are derided as "isolationists."

But we say: Keep America the greatest power on earth, first on land, sea, in the air and space. Strike hard any enemy that strikes us. Hold high the torch of liberty, republicanism. But keep the bravest of America's young out of wars where no vital interest is at risk, and do not send our wealth abroad in foreign aid to balance the budgets of foreign regimes when we cannot even balance our own.

This is not isolationism; it is Americanism. And if Clinton is set upon plunging us into Bosnia, we demand that Congress assert its rightful role in U.S. foreign policy and keep America out.

| *"An America whose military chases every ambulance will soon be unable to prevent the big calamities and . . . will soon exhaust Americans' tolerance even for seeing to little contingencies."*

THE UNITED STATES SHOULD ONLY INTERVENE IN MAJOR WARS

John Hillen

John Hillen is a defense policy analyst at the Heritage Foundation, a conservative public policy think tank. In the following viewpoint, Hillen argues that U.S. resources are limited and, therefore, the United States is unable to continue in its role as the lead protector of global security. He maintains that U.S. allies must begin to take responsibility for peacemaking and humanitarian aid in regional conflicts so that the U.S. military can focus its attention on major wars that are of vital interest to the United States.

As you read, consider the following questions:

1. What are the three problems the United States must recognize if it is to avoid isolationism and wasteful activism in foreign affairs, according to the author?
2. According to Hillen, how should countries use the time between wars?
3. What are the primary functions of the U.S. defense policy, in the author's view?

Excerpted from John Hillen, "Superpowers Don't Do Windows," *Orbis*, Spring 1997. Reprinted by permission of JAI Press. *Footnotes in the original have been omitted in this reprint.*

Since the collapse of the Soviet Union, American foreign policy thinkers have been striving to define a role for the United States in the post–cold war world. Their proposals have ranged from "strategic independence" on the isolationist pole to "assertive multilateralism" and "benevolent hegemony" on the interventionist pole. The sheer volume of labels and taxonomies, far from suggesting a wealth of ideas, is clear evidence of what Jonathan Clarke dubbed America's "conceptual poverty."

"Superpowers Don't Do Windows"

Nonetheless, the majority of proposed post–cold war strategies appear to seek a sensible course that lays out an active international role for the United States as a global superpower while avoiding the dreaded specter of the "global cop"—wasting American lives and resources, tilting at windmills, and minding everyone's business but its own. Robert Tucker has called this quest for the middle road "the great issue of American foreign policy today. It is the contradiction between the persisting desire to remain the premier global power and an ever deepening aversion to bear the costs of this position." Another way to understand it is to consider Americans' desire for a reasonable policy of global engagement: one that preserves American involvement in global activities that benefit the United States but does not squander U.S. resources on global gendarmerie. As former secretary of defense James Schlesinger noted, "The reality of the post–Cold War world is that the U.S. has limited political capital for foreign ventures. . . . The clear inference is that we should husband that political capital for those matters that are of vital interest to the United States." To that end, Washington must promote a new security compact for America's alliances, for without substantial reworking to accommodate recent geopolitical and military trends, America's alliance system threatens to be a burden rather than a boon. Specifically, the system should demarcate a division of labor that takes advantage of allies' differing interests and military capabilities, with the fundamental dictum for the United States being, according to one government agent, "superpowers don't do windows." . . .

U.S. Interests Are Limited

The United States needs a flexible array of alliances to protect its interests around the globe. But however extensive and varied they may be, U.S. vital interests are finite. So, too, are U.S. resources. Hence, the critical questions that any new strategy must address are where, when, why, and how the United States ought to be willing and able to intervene militarily—and where, when, why, and how it ought not to be willing to deploy its forces. In the post–cold war world, perhaps the best metaphor for the proper U.S. role in alliances is the role the Mayo Clinic plays in health affairs, or the FBI plays in law enforcement. That is, the United States should take the lead in the hierarchy of global security, but within a cooperative system in which allies play supporting roles. The Mayo Clinic and the FBI undertake only those essential duties that are in keeping with their unique talents and resources, leaving routine health care and law enforcement to local hospitals and police. For otherwise, those elite agencies would not only drown in minutiae and waste their resources, they would soon lose their capacity to perform the challenging tasks for which they were formed.

If the United States is to avoid both damaging isolationism and wasteful activism in foreign affairs, it must recognize that it cannot and should not attempt to do everything. That means America should focus on security problems in its "jurisdiction," leaving its allies and like-minded states to play the roles of local doctor and cop. The United States also must recognize that it, and it alone, can perform the unique, expensive, and demanding task of deterring or defeating major-power aggression in any region of the globe. To maintain the skills necessary to execute this function requires strategy, doctrine, training, and force structure focused on deterrence and war fighting, not on peacekeeping missions. Lastly, the United States must realize that a failure to be prepared to combat serious security threats will sooner or later have consequences so catastrophic as to dwarf the problems of muddling through a Bosnia-, Haiti-, or Somalia-type mission.

STRETCHED TO THE LIMIT

Unilateral disarmament is a recurring pattern in American history, and the post–cold war years are no exception. Since 1991, the U.S. military has suffered at least a 35 percent decrease in both force structure and defense funding. As a result, the force is the smallest fielded by the nation since 1940. Unfortunately, these slashing cuts have occurred only on the supply side. On the demand side—commitments overseas—the military has actually been saddled with new responsibilities. In short, the U.S. armed forces, like so many downsized institutions, are being asked to do more with less, leading to two severe consequences. The first is a disparity between stated U.S. security commitments and the forces fielded by the nation, which has been the focus of intense debates. The second is the resulting strain (on both personnel and matériel) the armed forces suffer as they attempt to compensate with an accelerated operational tempo. Their effort to do so has deprived the armed services of a prudent balance among current operations, training, readiness, and funding for future operations and equipment, owing primarily to overseas deployment requirements for the myriad missions they are asked to perform. For instance, on any given day in 1996 the army had some 105,000 soldiers permanently stationed overseas and another 40,000 on temporary duty in some sixty countries. This demand, coupled with reductions in force size, means that many soldiers are deploying at a rate 300–400 percent higher than during the cold war. In a time of relative peace, nearly 15 percent of active-duty army soldiers are deployed on twelve-month hardship tours of duty. A General Accounting Office (GAO) investigation in fact found that some army units were deployed more than 210 days per year. . . .

These requirements are literally wearing out men and matériel, and former Pentagon planner Robert Gaskin has noted that the military is "approaching burnout." The high rate of current operations has strained budgets, equipment, and units to the point where all services have canceled required wartime training exercises. In one such instance, peacekeeping support duties in 1995 forced three air force fighter wings to cancel critical combat training exercises. As a result of these trade-offs, 28 percent of the services' frequently deployed units are not combat ready.". . .

History suggests that military powers should use the breathing space between major conflicts to replenish their military stocks, train (and rest) their personnel, and aggressively experiment with new doctrines and equipment. Instead, the U.S. military is being driven into the ground by an already high operating tempo compounded by a series of peripheral peace operations. Speaker of the House Newt Gingrich (R-Ga.) has recognized that this effort is "stretching our military [to] the verge of the breaking point." He noted that

> at some point somebody needs to stand up and say there is a minimum size to being the world's only superpower, and we have gotten smaller than that in terms of our regular units, and we have an obligation to insist on a military in which people can serve without being burned out by the sheer constancy of their being used.

DIVERGING MILITARY COMPETENCIES

. . . The International Institute for Strategic Studies (IISS) recently concluded that "without the US, European North Atlantic Treaty

Organization (NATO) member-states do not have the capability to mount a combined arms operation of more than 30,000 troops, with air and naval support, capable of engaging in a full-scale military conflict outside NATO borders." Moreover, the core competencies of the American military and those of America's allies are diverging. While the United States focuses on deterrence and war fighting, many of its allies are refocusing their shrinking militaries on peacekeeping and operations other than war. . . .

With decreasing support available from allies, the United States must continue to fund, provide, and train large forces for the war-fighting capabilities needed to protect the vital interests of America and its allies. That is why America's regional allies must take the lead in future Somalias, Haitis, and Bosnias—missions of regional peacekeeping, crisis management, and humanitarian relief—so as to leave the United States free to focus its energies on global power projection and large-scale combat operations.

DIVERGING INTERESTS

American partnership with regional powers expected to play the role of "the cop on the beat" is not a novel idea. The Nixon Doctrine rested in part on such devolution of responsibility to certain states, like Iran under the shah, on the assumption that these locally powerful allies could spare the United States the need to intervene directly. But in those days of cold war, a commonly perceived threat made for a confluence of interests between the United States and its allies. Today the situation is very different, and as the Iraq crisis of September 1996 highlighted, even a Saddam Hussein is not enough to ensure common cause in a key region. If anything, the latest round of confrontations with Iraq underscored an historical truism: alliances and coalitions tend to weaken as soon as the perception of threat diminishes. Thus, in comparison with his aggression against Kuwait and threat to the entire Arabian peninsula, Saddam's limited assault on an Iraqi Kurdish faction in August and September of 1996 elicited vastly different responses—the unilateral U.S. cruise-missile strike was unsupported or openly criticized by close allies such as France, Turkey, and Saudi Arabia. Similarly, during the cold war, the overwhelming threat posed by the Warsaw Pact was the centripetal force holding NATO together. Today, absent that unifying threat, the stakes in local crises such as that in Bosnia are different for the United States and Europe. Bosnia may be the primary European security problem and it may touch the vital national interests of European powers, but it is not a primary concern of the United States, and the large U.S.

engagement there serves only to erode the sole superpower's ability to discharge its primary functions.

THE PRIMARY FUNCTIONS

What are those functions? They are to prevent, deter, or confront security challenges of the first order—from the world's great military powers such as Russia and China—and of the second order—from aggressive and well-armed rogue regimes such as those in Iran, Iraq, and North Korea. Bosnia, while a compelling issue, is a third-order security challenge on the periphery of U.S. interests, and the U.S. commitment to do the heavy lifting for a peacekeeping force there only misconstrues the true American role in European and global security. The United States should be involved militarily, but in a supporting rather than a lead role.

PROTECTING AMERICA'S VITAL INTERESTS

When *should* we order our forces into combat?

The answer is clearest with countries our own size, for to war against them is to risk our national existence. We should not do so unless America's life is at stake. The Founding Fathers wrote not of dispatching invasion forces or of going to war, but of providing for the common defense; and historically, the United States did not go to war unless it thought itself attacked. For all of the moral fervor against Spanish rule in Cuba, it was not until Americans believed that Spain had sunk the battleship Maine that they clamored for war.

The coming of the Second World War taught us to take a larger view of self-defense. We saw that Hitler was picking off countries one by one, going from strength to strength as he exploited the resources of those he had conquered. If we had waited until he attacked us, it might have been too late. We applied this lesson in a muddled sort of way to containing the expansion of the Soviet sphere, taking stands in South Korea and South Vietnam as the only alternative to taking a stand closer to home. However wrong in its application to those two conflicts, the theory is sound: if necessary, we should fight to protect our *vital* interests abroad— those interests essential to our ability to protect ourselves.

David Fromkin, *New York Times Magazine*, February 27, 1994.

So far, most post–cold war security challenges have been well below the threshold of a major-power threat necessitating significant U.S. involvement and leadership. It follows that regional devolution should be implemented in handling local threats.

That is, allies closest to the problem and whose interests are most affected should be the prime movers in mitigating the threat and should not be overly dependent on an ally that may have little interest in addressing the crisis. An "all-for-one and one-for-all" approach to every security dilemma, no matter what size, does not make sense for U.S. alliances. Instead, Washington must promote structures, like NATO's new combined joint task force (CJTF), that empower regional allies to tackle local crises. As Owen Harries writes,

> In deciding when to deploy [military force], Washington should practice the sound federal principle of subsidiarity—that is, allowing problems to be handled at the level closest to the problem. This way, a sense of responsibility can be developed throughout the international system and the United States can reserve its own intentions for the great issues involving its vital interests, acting as a balancer of last resort rather than a busybody and bully.

However, America's cold war military alliances still dominate the international arena, and until other security apparatuses emerge, U.S.-led alliances are often the default mechanism for responding to local problems. In Bosnia NATO was called upon to solve the crisis, and the United States was thereby thrust into the political and military lead. But such quasi-military missions in areas of marginal importance are unpopular with the American public and offer little return for the investment of scarce national security resources. Many Americans question the utility of alliances in which the imperative of leadership forces the United States into operations and actions it might not otherwise undertake. That was the case in Bosnia, where preserving the credibility of NATO and the United States became the motivation for what Clinton administration officials characterized as a regrettable mission, the U.S.-led intervention. Clearly, the alliance and U.S. leadership were not functioning as the means to the ends of U.S. foreign policy, but became the end in themselves.

THE ALLIANCE SYSTEM MUST CHANGE

The confluence of these trends does not augur well for the continued management of international peace and security through an enduring alliance system. Alliances are intended to be a cost-effective means of protecting and promoting American interests. But the United States is no longer able to discriminate among security priorities, and the alliance system is hampering the effectiveness of U.S. national strategy. To reverse this slide, the United States must take charge of reforming the system instead of mistaking defense of the status quo as a manifestation of leadership.

Moreover, U.S. alliance leadership should not become a shibboleth for crisis management worldwide. Much as domestic policy analysts have questioned the utility of federal leadership in areas such as education and welfare, American foreign policy leadership should recognize a similar imperative in the global security hierarchy and not use America's leading role to usurp the responsibility, or discourage the capability, of alliance partners to take decisive action on minor regional affairs. . . .

REGIONAL POWERS MUST TAKE CHARGE

If the United States refrains from entering military alliances and takes no more than a supporting role in ethnic and religious conflicts or humanitarian disasters in most of the Third World, who will undertake these tasks? It is simply up to regional powers, with or without cooperation from the United Nations, to walk the beats in their neighborhoods. To the extent those powers need occasional U.S. assistance in logistics, intelligence, or other specialized capabilities, let them seek U.S. help, rather than vice versa. Let them ask Washington for an "alliance" or understanding, instead of the other way around. And the candidates for the roles of local leaders are obvious. In Latin America, the standouts are Argentina, Brazil, Chile, and Venezuela. In South Asia, India and Pakistan have no choice but to mend their fences or prepare to suffer forever. In Africa, the present prospects for regional leaders of any sort are dim. In the ex-Soviet world, the only possible policeman is, yes, Russia, assuming that unhappy country proves willing and able to take its place as a responsible regional power in league with the West. Filling out this roster of local "G.P.s" and "cops on the beat" may take many decades. But if there is to be a new world order, that is how it will come about, not through increased and indiscriminate American intervention, but through precisely the opposite. That is so, first, because an America whose military chases every ambulance will soon be unable to prevent the big calamities and, secondly, because it will soon exhaust Americans' tolerance even for seeing to little contingencies.

That does not mean the United States will not participate in lesser interventions that have clear goals and a chance for success. It also does not preclude aggressive U.S. diplomatic and economic strategies for those areas where the United States does not have a military alliance. Regional devolution, as an alliance strategy, merely means that all members should box at their own weight level to get the most out of the team.

AN INTERNATIONAL HIERARCHY

Most Americans would agree that the United States must be active in the world, but not so active that the effort wastes American resources and energies in interventions that yield little or no payoff and undermine military preparedness. The need for a policy of highly selective engagement is all the more acute owing to the numerous security challenges that the United States must address with a shrinking pool of military resources. There is just no alternative, therefore, to reforming U.S. alliances in ways that forestall further confusion about the U.S. role in minor post–cold war security challenges. The way to begin is simply to announce to America's allies and partners the criteria that will define when, where, why, and how the United States might choose to use military force and, by implication, the situations in which it will expect its partners to assume leadership. In other words, America proclaims that "superpowers don't do windows," so if you want your local windows washed, you had better gear up to do them yourselves.

Such an "agonizing reappraisal" might shock some, especially in Europe, but it is based on a commonsense recognition that there is a hierarchy in international security composed of local military powers, regional powers, global powers, superpowers, and entities such as alliances and international organizations. The hierarchy conduces to order rather than chaos when each constituent part has roles and responsibilities that match its interests and capabilities. If an organization tries to do too much, it fails. That has been evident for the past few years with the United Nations. Similarly, if the United States attempts to do too much, as it does now, its forces become overstretched and lose sight of their most significant roles.

Consequently, the United States should focus its security policies on major threats such as other great powers or rogue regimes that can upset the balance of power in key regions. America's allies should take the lead in local crisis management, peacekeeping, and humanitarian relief operations. History shows that another major conflict is never far away and is usually unpredictable. The United States is the only nation capable of forestalling or fighting that conflict. It must remain focused on doing so, for that is the task no one else can do.

| "Without question, an American response always must be planned carefully and usually should take place within an international consensus."

U.S. Intervention Should Be Part of a Multinational Effort

Robert H. Phinny

Robert H. Phinny argues in the following viewpoint that if American interests are endangered by the actions of another country, then the United States must respond to that threat. However, he contends, few actions require a unilateral defense by the United States. Most interventions should be multinational efforts organized through the United Nations, he maintains. Phinny is the former U.S. ambassador to the Kingdom of Swaziland.

As you read, consider the following questions:
1. In the author's opinion, why is the United States precluded from turning the responsibility for peacekeeping over to the United Nations?
2. What steps should the United States take when its interests are threatened, according to Phinny?
3. What limits should be placed on peacekeeping forces, in Phinny's view?

Reprinted from Robert H. Phinny, "A Global Referee Must Plot Each Response Carefully," *San Diego Union-Tribune*, Editorial, March 25, 1995, by permission of the author.

No matter how dangerous or baffling a crisis in a sovereign country is, if it threatens an important national interest, then the United States must respond.

The key question is: How?

It is not an idle question because we can foresee future challenges to American interests, not to mention the current ones in Bosnia, Somalia, Haiti and elsewhere. For instance, as the Castro regime in Cuba comes to an end, and as important regional powers such as Zaire confront internal misgovernance and deep tribal animosities, the United States once again will find it has to respond.

THE AMERICAN RESPONSE

Without question, an American response always must be planned carefully and usually should take place within an international consensus.

U.S. military power should only be brought to bear unilaterally when there is a direct threat to clearly vital American interests, such as a direct attack of American territory or our most important economic lifelines.

When we confront challenges like Saddam Hussein's threat to the flow of petroleum from the Persian Gulf, it is right for the United States to exercise strong leadership and be prepared to commit substantial U.S. military forces.

But even in this type of case, it is preferable to operate within an international consensus. President George Bush's brilliant mobilization of the world community behind the Persian Gulf effort meant that we were able to isolate Iraq, deliver "the mother of all defeats," keep Saddam in check thereafter and ensure a degree of stability in the gulf.

However, most international dangers to the United States are not as sharply outlined as Saddam's challenge. It is as clear to me—as to any American—that the current threats center on areas where civil war is in full swing or where government, conventionally defined, has broken down or disappeared, resulting in enormous suffering and threats to regional stability. Nations such as Bosnia, Somalia, Haiti and Rwanda are good examples.

It has proven particularly difficult to forge a consensus in the United States on how to deal with the threat of disruption in distant and remote areas of the world.

Neither the recent Republican [Bush] nor the current Democratic [Clinton] administration has succeeded in forging a fresh consensus. Our intellectual and media communities have been divided over the nature of the proper American response. This likely will continue to be the case for some time.

At the same time, America's responsibility in times of world crises, and the burdens of peacekeeping, will continue to weigh heavily and will be a source of enormous public and political debate. We have not the interest, desire, or the resources to be the world's policeman.

THE BURDEN MUST BE SHARED

We cannot afford to abandon either peace-keeping or a multilateral approach to solving difficult problems. As much as we would wish otherwise, conflicts are going to continue. The world is going to look to the United States for leadership. It will be in our interests to provide that leadership, but we cannot and should not bear the full burden alone.

Madeleine K. Albright, *U.S. Department of State Dispatch*, November 15, 1993.

Moreover, if we are to sustain American actions in the post–Cold War world and make them count, we have to find ways to share with other nations the responsibility for maintaining stability. This means almost always acting within an international consensus.

We cannot go to the other extreme and dump the threats of Bosnia, the Caucasus region or Africa in the lap of the United Nations and walk away ourselves. The United Nations, after all, is no more than a collection of nations and we are part of that collective body. Having no money or forces of its own, the United Nations cannot act to keep the peace without Security Council agreement, and we are one of five permanent members of the council.

THE STEPS TO TAKE

In almost all significant threats to the peace, American decisions and actions, be it diplomatic, material or military, will be key in defining strategy or carrying out actions within the U.N. framework or outside.

• The first step that the United States always must take, in the face of a dangerous international situation, is to mobilize our intelligence (its assets and analysis) to determine: 1) the facts, and 2) the likely outcomes.

• Second, when it comes time to act, the first and preferred form of American action is diplomatic. That action includes the shaping of an international coalition. In almost all cases a Security Council mandate is necessary.

• Third, if simple persuasion and diplomatic action do not produce a settlement, then pressure must be brought on the contestants to end their confrontation. Political isolation is one such technique. Also useful are financial sanctions and arms embargoes.

But in the absence of a political settlement, an economic embargo by itself will not suffice. We have embargoed Cuba for decades and, despite the end of the Soviet influence, Castro, although weakened, is still in power.

• Fourth, no crisis we have faced in recent years is without its humanitarian consequences, and we have to be prepared to deal with them.

• The last step we should contemplate in dealing with a crisis is military action. Enforcing embargoes and providing humanitarian relief can draw on American military assets, but other uses of military power should be held in reserve until absolutely necessary.

PEACEKEEPING

When we reach the point that military force is required, the best means is peacekeeping. Again, an international effort is the right way to go. But deploying military forces in the cause of peacekeeping should only be undertaken when the diplomats, together with the parties to the dispute, have defined a political objective.

As all of us have learned from Bosnia, when no political objective has been agreed upon, it is extremely dangerous to dispatch armed forces with limited means to protect themselves.

But when there is a solid political understanding, as was the case in Cambodia, peacekeepers in limited numbers can be effectively deployed.

In any case, peacekeepers ought not to be dispatched in an open-ended engagement. Their involvement should be time limited and subject to frequent review by the United Nations, or whatever ad hoc coalition exists to support them.

"To stand by in the face of mass slaughter debases our nation's principles and insults our collective conscience."

THE UNITED STATES SHOULD INTERVENE TO PREVENT MASSIVE LOSS OF LIFE

Stephen J. Solarz and Michael E. O'Hanlon

The United States should intervene in other countries' wars not only if they affect U.S. interests, but also to provide humanitarian aid or to prevent a massive loss of life, argue Stephen J. Solarz and Michael E. O'Hanlon in the following viewpoint. The United States must take the primary responsibility to prevent genocide, the authors contend, because to ignore it is morally reprehensible and because no other countries are in a position to take the lead role. Solarz is the vice chairman of the International Crisis Group, an advocacy organization for war-torn countries. O'Hanlon is a military analyst with the Brookings Institution, a public policy think tank in Washington, D.C.

As you read, consider the following questions:

1. In what two countries should the United States have led a humanitarian mission that might have saved hundreds of thousands of lives, according to Solarz and O'Hanlon?
2. According to the authors, what two criteria should be used to determine if the United States should provide humanitarian intervention in the world's conflicts?
3. In the authors' opinion, what was the most important goal of the intervention in Somalia?

Excerpted from Stephen J. Solarz and Michael E. O'Hanlon, "Humanitarian Intervention: When Is Force Justified?" *The Washington Quarterly*, vol. 20, no. 4 (Autumn 1997), pp. 3–14; ©1997 by the Center for Strategic and International Studies (CSIS) and the Massachusetts Institute of Technology. Reprinted by permission of MIT Press. *Endnotes in the original have been omitted in this reprint.*

W hen, if ever, should the United States participate in forcible military interventions for the primary purpose of saving lives in situations where vital U.S. interests are not at stake? This question has emerged as among the most contentious in post–Cold War U.S. security policy. There is a clear national consensus that the U.S. military cannot and should not be the world's police force. We have neither the will nor the ability to respond with military force to the bulk of armed conflicts—most of them wars within rather than between states—currently being waged or likely to be fought in the future.

U.S. HUMANITARIAN INTERVENTION IS NECESSARY

Fortunately, there is no reason to consider forcible military intervention to save lives in most civil conflicts around the world today. The scale and pace of killing, however regrettable, are generally too low to justify the inevitably expensive and dangerous application of outside military force—always a blunt instrument of policy and peacemaking. The most compelling recent example of where U.S.-led forcible humanitarian intervention was called for was Rwanda in 1994; there, it would have been possible for a modestly sized international force with robust rules of engagement to have saved the lives of hundreds of thousands of otherwise-defenseless Tutsis and moderate Hutus. Another prominent example of a humanitarian intervention being consistent with these criteria was in Somalia in 1992; the introduction of U.S.-led forces saved tens of thousands if not hundreds of thousands of Somalis who would otherwise have starved to death.

Our basic argument is that the United States should be prepared to intervene militarily to prevent the massive loss of life, wherever it may be occurring, provided that a multilateral and militarily sound mission to do so can be devised at moderate risk to the troops that would carry it out. The main argument against such interventions is that they will inevitably lead to a growing and perpetual military involvement in dozens of countries around the world. But situations that truly require a forcible U.S. military role arise fairly infrequently. Intervening to stop large-scale humanitarian catastrophes will not produce a slippery slope that leads to playing the role of the world's police force because there are, at any time, few cases in which tens or hundreds of thousands of people are actually at imminent risk of death. As of this writing in mid-1997, in fact, there appear to be none. Over the past year or so, only Burundi and eastern Zaire have been close to such a threshold.

In most of the world's conflict zones—such as those in Afghanistan, Turkey, Kashmir, Cyprus, Burma (Myanmar), Peru, Colombia, and others—the death rate from civil strife is often comparable in per capita terms to the annual murder rate in the United States of roughly 1,000 per 10 million inhabitants (see table). Although such a level of violence is highly regrettable, it is simply not enough to justify the risk and cost of outside military intervention to force an end to the killing. (Nevertheless, humanitarian imperatives combined with other critical factors, such as a U.S. interest in promoting hemispheric democracy and stemming drug and refugee flows into this country, *can* justify intervention in cases in which moral considerations alone might not. This was the case in both Haiti and Panama in recent years.)

In short, the worry that humanitarian interventions constitute a "slippery slope" that risks involving U.S. military forces in the world's problems is misplaced. If U.S. policymakers follow a clear set of criteria—the existence or risk of truly massive starvation or genocide, and the clear ability of outside forces to make a difference—they can narrow the list of candidates for intervention to at most a very few. The notion that there are dozens of equally sensible peacekeeping missions waiting to swallow U.S. military resources and readiness is simply wrong.

THE RATIONALE FOR HUMANITARIAN INTERVENTION

Some will argue that the men and women of today's U.S. armed forces should not be asked to risk their lives for purely humanitarian reasons. Only when the vital interests of the country are at stake, so the argument goes, should we be prepared to run the risk of combat casualties. But the values of the United States are not so neatly separable from its interests. To stand by in the face of mass slaughter debases our nation's principles and insults our collective conscience. Accordingly, recent polls indicate that the American people will support military efforts to stop genocide by roughly a 2-to-1 margin, even at some risk to U.S. troops and even in the aftermath of the 1993 tragedy in Mogadishu. [Eighteen U.S. soldiers were killed when the humanitarian aid mission turned into a hunt for a Somali warlord.] Tolerating genocide also lessens the moral authority that other countries accord the United States. That in turn could make them less inclined to follow our leadership on matters of more narrow U.S. national interest. . . .

THE NEED FOR U.S. COMBAT TROOPS

Even if humanitarian intervention makes sense on moral grounds, why must the United States—a country that already provides general strategic stability for the international community through its global military capabilities—take the primary responsibility for conducting it?

The answer is that virtually no other country is in a position to do so. In some cases, Britain or France or the two together may be able to play the lead role, but they face serious military constraints in areas such as strategic transport that preclude rapid response during the early days or weeks of a massive humanitarian tragedy. Most other countries do not have the physical means even to initiate a forcible humanitarian intervention, and they often lack the necessary international consciousness and political confidence as well. Unless the world's leading power considers the stakes sufficiently high and the prospects sufficiently promising to put its own armed forces at risk, other states will stay on the sidelines too—at least until a cease-fire is negotiated and a United Nations (UN) Chapter VI peacekeeping mission, based on the acquiescence of all parties to the conflict in question, becomes possible. . . .

ONLY THE UNITED STATES HAS THE NECESSARY ASSETS

To have the capacity for autonomous operations in an austere environment, a division-size force of crack infantry soldiers would usually be the minimum required for a forcible humanitarian intervention. These troops would need assets such as communications systems able to contact national command structures, engineering and medical units, helicopter transport teams, and other capabilities not always found within brigades. A number of small North Atlantic Treaty Organization (NATO) countries acting together might have the requisite combat power and competence to carry out a forcible humanitarian intervention, but they would probably lack the necessary transport and logistics for rapid and extensive overseas operations. States such as Israel, Taiwan, and South Korea would be constrained for the same reasons—and also because they face acute threats in their own neighborhoods that preclude them from the strategic luxury of participating in operations that address less immediate risks to their national security. The time may come when an African rapid-reaction force and other regional structures can assume some of the responsibilities for these types of operations in their areas. But that day is probably even further off than for the smaller European countries, given the difficulties of the task and the cost of equipping units for autonomous operations on foreign soil. Until others can do more, the U.S. role will remain crucial. . . .

Consider the case of Bosnia. Whatever the merits of an early and massive intervention with ground forces to reimpose a unified Bosnian state, it might well have incited dedicated Serb guerrilla resistance against outside forces and led to far greater casualties than Western publics would have been willing to accept. An intervention with those purposes probably would have been too ambitious. On the other hand, operations to stop the momentum of ethnic cleansing by driving Serb forces from specific tracts of land through a combination of Western air power and Bosnian-Croat ground offensives clearly were possible. Combined Croat-Muslim forces demonstrated that fact in late 1995. Also, the earlier use of air strikes to destroy the artillery used in ethnic-cleansing operations or to break the siege of Sarajevo could have helped to protect populations and facilitate peace talks—just as it ultimately did in the months before the Dayton conference. [Dayton, Ohio, was where the 1995 Bosnian peace agreement was signed.]

The U.S.-led operation in Somalia illustrates even more clearly the importance of a properly designed intervention. Its humanitarian side worked much better than did its political one. The original mission, to end widespread starvation caused by fighting that hindered the distribution of relief supplies, was both an immediate and an enduring success. Morally, it was also the most important goal of the operation. Additional efforts at catalyzing a Somali political reconciliation process and protecting that process, though well-intentioned and designed in part to stabilize the humanitarian situation, were a notable failure. Perhaps they could have worked—but only with much greater resolve and clarity of purpose on the part of the international community in 1993. Absent those elements, it would have been much wiser to limit the operation to its original goal.

THE UNDERLYING PROBLEMS

The received wisdom about humanitarian operations has been that they must "solve the underlying problems"—in other words, that peacekeeping without nation-building is futile. We are directly challenging that guideline in cases of extreme humanitarian urgency. Political reconciliation and stabilization are always desirable. But confidence that they will be achieved in a given case should not be a prerequisite to stopping genocides or manmade humanitarian catastrophe.

Another example where fundamental political reform would have been difficult, but where intervention was militarily justifiable and morally obligatory, was Rwanda in 1994. The scale and pace of the atrocities were nearly unimaginable: In 100 days,

WAR-RELATED DEATHS AROUND THE WORLD

(conflicts with an annual death rate of 1,000 or more as of early-mid 1996)

Country or Region	Major Cause of Casualties	Total Deaths	Annual Death Rate	Death Rate Ratio to U.S. Murder Rate[1]	Thousands of Fighters[2]
Afghanistan 1990–	Civil War	15,000+	5,000	3:1	50
Algeria 1992–	Insurgency	40,000	5,000	2:1	150 vs. 12
Burundi 1993–	Acts of Genocide	150,000	50,000	80:1	15
Burma/ Myanmar 1993–	War against Two Insurgencies	1,000+	1,000	1:5	286 vs. 20
Russia 1994–	War against Chechen Resistance	30,000+	20,000+	150:1 (in Chechnya)	40 vs. 5
Rwanda 1994–	Genocide, War, then Sporadic Warfare	500,000+	1,000	1:1	40 vs. 20
Somalia 1991–	Civil War	350,000	1,000	1:1	10 vs. 10
Turkey 1984–	War against Kurd Insurgency	15,000+	3,000	1:2	600 vs. 10

Notes: [1] Ratio compares per capita death rate during conflict to annual U.S. murder rate (approximately 1,000 per 10 million). [2] The column for numbers of fighters shows government forces first.

Stephen J. Solarz and Michael E. O'Hanlon, *Washington Quarterly*, Autumn 1997.

---

more than half a million Tutsis and moderate Hutus were hacked to death by extremist mobs, generally armed only with machetes. A competent infantry force could have subdued the murderous minions of the Hutu extremists; indeed, the UN peacekeeping commander on the scene at the time, Canadian Gen. Romeo Dallaire, believed the worst of the killings could have been prevented had his 2,500-strong force been augmented to a total size between 5,000 and 8,000. Instead, his force was reduced to 270 soldiers, a number far too small to prevent the ensuing genocide. Even if 10,000 or 20,000 troops had been needed, the United States and other concerned countries should have acted. It does not seem an exaggeration to say that their unwillingness to respond to General Dallaire's recommendation will go down as one of the international community's greatest moral failures in the last half century. . . .

ACCEPTING THE RESPONSIBILITY

Over the next decade and beyond, countries other than the United States must get better at operations to protect innocent civilians threatened by warfare around the world. This is a mission that might someday be entrusted to an enlarged and enhanced NATO—and perhaps ultimately to a UN force consisting of dedicated military units from various countries. But for now the greatest responsibility falls on the United States, and it is a responsibility that we can and should accept. . . .

As a signatory of the 1949 Genocide Convention, the United States is already legally obliged to address that specific category of war-related humanitarian tragedy. But its national values and interests provide an even more compelling and sweeping rationale for intervening to stop massive violence-related death. As the endorsements of operations in northern Iraq, Haiti, and Somalia indicate, a now widely accepted doctrine of humanitarian intervention legitimates the United States and other countries in doing so—despite the arguments of those who assert that the right of national sovereignty is supreme over all others and precludes the international community from taking such actions.

One of the great and enduring lessons of this century involves the depths of depravity to which the human spirit can sink. We cannot bring back to life the victims of the Holocaust and the other genocides that have been among the cardinal characteristics of the century in which we live. But if we can resolve to prevent future genocides and mass killings when possible, the sacrifices and sufferings of those who lost their lives in the gas chambers of Nazi-occupied Europe and the killing fields of Cambodia and Rwanda will not have been entirely in vain.

"Forward deployed U.S. forces . . . are vital to regional stability and to keeping these crises from escalating into full-scale wars."

A STRONG U.S. MILITARY PRESENCE ENSURES WORLD PEACE

Charles C. Krulak and Jay L. Johnson

Charles C. Krulak and Jay L. Johnson argue in the following viewpoint that a strong U.S. military presence overseas is essential to maintain peace in unstable regions. These troops can help prevent and deter small wars before they break out, the authors assert, as well as resolve or terminate crises after they erupt. Maintaining a U.S. military force overseas is a small "peace insurance premium" to pay for preventing a small conflict from becoming a major war, Krulak and Johnson contend. Krulak is the thirty-first commandant of the U.S. Marine Corps. Johnson is the twenty-sixth chief of naval operations for the U.S. Navy.

As you read, consider the following questions:

1. According to the authors, what measures did U.S. expeditionary forces take between 1994 and 1996 to resolve crises in unstable regions around the world?
2. In Krulak and Johnson's opinion, how does a failure to respond to world crises encourage more serious crises in the future?
3. How are world crises similar to forest fires, in the authors' opinion?

Reprinted from Charles C. Krulak and Jay L. Johnson, "A 'Forward Presence' in a Violent World," *The Washington Times*, November 25, 1996, p. A19, by permission of *The Washington Times*.

This morning, keys are turning in the front doors of thousands of American business offices "forward deployed" literally all over the world. American companies invest in overseas presence because actually "being there" is clearly the best way to do business.

A MILITARY FORWARD PRESENCE

Also this morning, United States Navy amphibious assault ships carrying 4,400 combat-ready American Marines are forward deployed in the waters of the Mediterranean Sea and the Persian Gulf. And at sea in the Mediterranean and in the Persian Gulf are aircraft carrier battle groups with 16,000 sailors and two air wings of combat ready aircraft. And finally, in the Far East, the United States has permanently deployed a third aircraft carrier battle group and a third amphibious ready group. The vigilant "forward presence" of these forces is vital, but not always as visible to Americans as it is to the rest of the world. Their routine daily efforts don't always make the headlines, but they are vitally important to world peace and stability.

Some argue that the forward presence these forces represent is no longer necessary. They argue that forces reacting from the United States are enough to maintain international stability. They further maintain that "brushfires", or outbreaks of regional instability, are insignificant, or incidental at best. And they argue that America can no longer afford the forward presence of these forces on what amounts to a near continuous basis.

We would argue just the opposite. Forward deployed U.S. forces, primarily naval expeditionary forces—the Navy-Marine Corps team—are vital to regional stability and to keeping these crises from escalating into full-scale wars. To those who argue that the United States can't afford to have this degree of vigilance anymore, we say: The United States can't afford not to.

THE BRUSHFIRES WILL CONTINUE

These brushfires, whether the result of long-standing ethnic tensions or resurgent nationalism in the wake of the Cold War, will only continue. The Cold War was an anomaly.

Never again will we live in a bipolar world whose nuclear shadow suppressed nationalism and ethnic tensions. We have, in some respects, reverted back to the world our ancestors knew: A world in disorder. Somalia, Bosnia, Liberia, Haiti, Rwanda, Iraq and the Taiwan Straits are merely examples of the types of continuing crises we now face. Some might call this period an age of chaos.

143

The United States and the world cannot afford to allow any crisis to escalate into threats to the United States', and the world's, vital interests. And while the skies are not dark with smoke from these brushfires, today's world demands a new approach. The concepts of choice must be selective and committed engagement, unencumbered global operations and prompt crisis resolution. There is no better way to maintain and enforce these concepts than with the forward presence of the U.S. Navy-Marine Corps team.

PREVENT, DETER, RESOLVE, TERMINATE

There are four basic tenets to international security in today's world: Prevention, deterrence, crisis resolution, and war termination. The underlying assumption of these tenets is that the U.S. and its allies should not be forced into winning a war in an overwhelming (and expensive) fashion. Instead, it is much better— and cheaper—to resolve a crisis before it burns out of control.

• Prevent: The key to prevention is continuous presence in a region. This lets our friends know we have an interest and lets potential foes know that we're there to check any move. Both effects occur without any direct action taken. Although hard to measure, the psychological impact of naval expeditionary forces is undeniable. This regional presence underwrites political and economic stability.

This is forward presence.

• Deter: Presence does not prevent every crisis. Some rogues are going to be tempted to strike no matter what the odds, and will require active measures to be deterred. When crises reach this threshold, there is no substitute for sustained actual presence. Naval expeditionary forces can quickly take on the role of the very visible fist. Friends and potential enemies recognize naval expeditionary forces as capable of defending or destroying them. This visible fist, free from diplomatic and territorial constraints, forms the bedrock of regional deterrence. For example, the mere presence of naval expeditionary forces deterred Chinese attempts to derail the democratic process in Taiwan and countered Iraqi saber-rattling toward Jordan. It's hard to quantify the cost savings of deterring a crisis before it requires our intervention. But the savings are real—in dollars, and often in blood and human misery.

This is forward presence.

• Resolve: If a crisis can be neither prevented nor deterred, then prompt and decisive crisis resolution is imperative before the crisis threatens vital interests. U.S. naval expeditionary forces are a transoceanic key that finds and opens—forcibly if necessary—any gateway into a fiery world. This ability is equally expandable and retractable according to the situation. Perhaps most importantly, naval expeditionary forces don't need permission from foreign governments to be on scene and take unilateral action in a crisis. This both unencumbers the force and takes pressure off allies to host any outside forces.

Between 1994 and 1996, for example, U.S. naval expeditionary forces simultaneously and unilaterally deployed to Liberia and to the Central African Republic (1,500 miles inland) to protect U.S. and international citizens. They also launched measured retaliatory Tomahawk strikes to constrain unacceptable Iraqi behavior, and conducted naval air and Tomahawk strikes which brought the warring parties in Bosnia to the negotiating table.

This is forward presence.

AMERICA MUST FILL THE VACUUM OF POWER

Foreign policy does not exist in a vacuum; it must have military capability to protect and project it. Diplomacy without power is a prayer—not to God, but to one's adversary, and its fulfillment depends on the mood and whim of the party prayed to. . . .

America's interest in regional stability cannot be ignored. If America's presence and purpose in the world can be doubted, if we tolerate vacuums of power, they will be filled by others, and ultimately American blood will be spilled. In the past century, we have been called upon time and again to secure peace and liberty after our leaders thought the world no longer needed us.

Malcolm Wallop, "Beyond the Water's Edge," *Policy Review*, Fall 1995.

• Terminate: Each of the above tenets is worthy of the United States paying an annual peace insurance premium. Otherwise we, and our allies, risk paying the emotional, physical and financial costs of a full-blown conflagration that began as just another brushfire. If there is a war, naval expeditionary forces will be first to fight. They are inherently capable of enabling the follow-on forces from the United States for as long as it takes. And they will remain on-scene to enforce the settlement that ends the conflict.

This is forward presence.

The Iraqs, Central Africas, Somalias and Bosnias inevitably destabilize and erode world order and respect for the rule of law. Indeed, a failure to respond to them encourages future—more serious—crises.

A Small Price to Pay

The United States must foster stability around the world, today and tomorrow. The peace insurance premium is a small price and is the cost of leadership. Who else is capable of this type of forward presence on a global basis? For the United States, maintaining a steady commitment to stability will be a challenge. But maintain it we must, or the price, literally and figuratively, will be much greater down the road.

The example of fighting forest fires is precisely applicable. The philosophy is simple: Prevention through living in the environment; deterrence through vigilance; and resolution through quick and selective engagement. Ninety-five percent of all forest fires are contained—the direct result of the watchful presence of the local initial attack crews who attack flashpoints. As for the other 5 percent, once the window of opportunity for decisive early action is missed, firefighters must be brought in from outside the region, and it is exponentially more expensive. Sometimes there are casualties—casualties that would not have been incurred had the fire been contained before it had the opportunity to flare.

America's Navy-Marine Corps team is underway, ready and on-scene at trouble spots around the world. Forward presence makes it—and will keep it—the right force, tailor-made for these uncertain and sometimes fiery times.

> "In situations where words are likely
> to be ignored but soldiers are
> unlikely to be sent, without
> economic sanctions the policymaker's
> quiver would be empty."

THE UNITED STATES SHOULD IMPOSE ECONOMIC SANCTIONS

Elliott Abrams

Many countries impose sanctions on other countries in an attempt to pressure them to change their policies. Sanctions can be economic, such as restricting foreign aid or trade; political, such as closing embassies or expelling foreign nationals; or military, such as arms embargoes. In the following viewpoint, Elliott Abrams argues that the imposition of sanctions is an effective way to express displeasure at another country's conduct. Furthermore, he maintains, economic sanctions are effective at changing the country's undesirable behavior. Eliminating economic sanctions as a foreign policy tool would leave a government with only two choices, Abrams contends: words—denunciations, which are easy to ignore—or war. As a global leader, the United States should set the standard and continue to impose sanctions against its adversaries, he asserts. Abrams is the president of Ethics and Public Policy Center, a Washington, D.C.–based think tank.

As you read, consider the following questions:

1. According to Abrams, when are words effective as a foreign policy tool?
2. In the author's opinion, why are multilateral sanctions rarely achieved?

Excerpted from Elliott Abrams, "Words or War: Why Sanctions Are Necessary," *The Weekly Standard*, July 27, 1998. Reprinted by permission of *The Weekly Standard*.

In rhetoric not ordinarily heard from the business community, the new lobby known as USA☆Engage warns that "two-thirds of the world's population" is now "threatened" by a novel form of "proliferation." The threat that alarms USA☆Engage is not the proliferation of, say, ballistic missiles, but the spread of trade sanctions imposed by the U.S. government.

SANCTIONS ARE UNDER ATTACK

Indeed, the explicit goal of the several hundred businesses and trade associations that make up USA*Engage is to end the use of sanctions as a tool of U.S. foreign and security policy. In an extraordinary media and advertising campaign in recent months, USA*Engage, the Chamber of Commerce, the National Foreign Trade Council, the National Association of Manufacturers, and other business lobbies have worked to discredit sanctions as a blunt, overused instrument that only does harm. Responding in part to this pressure, the Senate moved to lift sanctions on India and Pakistan and to weaken the force of existing and future sanctions by exempting agricultural and medical goods. A bill sponsored by Sen. Richard Lugar that would have largely gutted all future sanctions—the favored legislation of the anti-sanctions crusaders—was only narrowly turned back. Lugar's bill may well resurface after a Senate task force issues its report on the issue.

As this burgeoning campaign to abolish them makes clear, sanctions are a great annoyance to the constituents of America's business lobbies. While foreign competitors, French or Japanese or German, merrily bid for contracts abroad, American companies find themselves tangled in a web of legislation designed to express disapproval, block trade in certain commodities, or perhaps deny resources to disfavored or hostile regimes. But the elimination of economic sanctions as a foreign-policy tool would be an extraordinarily radical action, for it would leave our government facing its adversaries with just two alternatives: words or war.

A WAY TO REINFORCE WORDS

The history of U.S. human-rights policy shows that "mere" words can sometimes be effective tools. This is especially so when the regime under attack is pledged to respect common values, whether because it sees itself as part of the West and seeks American approval, as was the case with Latin American dictatorships over the past two decades, or because it has signed international agreements, as did the Soviet Union (which was pledged to the Universal Declaration of Human Rights and to the Helsinki Agreement). But words appear to have little impact on the most savage regimes, those we now call "pariah states," such as Libya and Iraq. Nor did words have much impact in past decades on the likes of Mussolini and Hitler. Confronted with hard cases, the United States may wish to reinforce its words with economic pressure.

Think of the policymaker's options. Country A is engaged in very grave human-rights abuses: a government-organized mob has killed some opposition leaders and burned down a church, and the government has jailed several honest judges and shot five journalists. Country B has been caught trying to send weapons-grade plutonium and missile-guidance systems to Iraq. Country C has just invaded an island belonging to its neighbor. We could simply denounce these acts from the podium in the State Department's press-briefing room. We could send troops to fight, as we did when Kuwait was overrun and when Grenada's government was hijacked. However, in situations where words are likely to be ignored but soldiers are unlikely to be sent, without economic sanctions the policymaker's quiver would be empty.

ECONOMIC PRESSURE

To escape the choice between words and war, governments for centuries have used economic pressure. Even when sanctions are mostly symbolic, they are still important, for they show that we take seriously what the regime in question is doing. More commonly, economic sanctions do have an economic effect on the targeted regime. And the proof is the fierce struggle by so many target governments to have the sanctions removed. They pay fortunes to lobbyists in Washington, and they denounce and revile the sanctions and the members of Congress who promote them—all the while insisting that the sanctions do not affect them in the least or that sanctions only starve children and do not hurt the regime. But with rare exceptions, American economic sanctions have a moral and an economic impact—and the target regimes deeply resent and are hurt by both.

UNILATERAL SANCTIONS

Opponents of U.S. sanctions have made "unilateral sanctions" their special target. They argue that sanctions observed by many nations would be much more effective. True enough. Far better for trade with an outlaw regime to be restricted by many nations than by just one. But the argument against unilateral sanctions has two great flaws.

The first is purely pragmatic. Like all forms of collective security, multilateral sanctions require a unanimity rarely achieved in international politics. . . .

WE MUST BE PREPARED TO ACT UNILATERALLY

It has become clear in Bosnia, Kosovo, Cyprus, Ireland, and has been clear for decades in the Middle East, that U.S. leadership on conflict resolution is essential. We have the responsibility to lead and we are not afraid to do so, even if it means, at times, that we act alone. But in the post Cold War world, we must also recognize that though we are an essential and indispensable force for peace and stability, we alone are not sufficient to resolve the world's pressing problems. We need the support and cooperation of like-minded nations. We can do a lot alone, and there will be times when we must act alone, but we can do a lot more with support from others. . . .

If we are unsuccessful in building a multilateral regime, and important national interests or core values are at issue, we must be prepared to act unilaterally. We cannot permit other countries to veto our use of sanctions by their failure to act. Our primary considerations in any eventual application of unilateral sanctions must be whether they are effective, whether they are part of a coherent strategy to change behavior, whether they contribute to or detract from our efforts to gain multilateral support for our policy objectives, and whether they are consistent with our international obligations and humanitarian principles. . . .

Sanctions should seek to influence, not simply to punish. Our measure of success must be effectiveness: what combination of measures can be assembled among like-minded countries to force or induce a change in the conduct of the offending state? That is, after all, the objective. If the best we can do is to act alone, so be it, but we owe it to the American people to exhaust other diplomatic measures first and have some reasonable prospect that our unilateral measures will have the intended effect.

Stuart E. Eizenstat, testimony before the House International Relations Committee, June 3, 1998.

The United States imposes economic sanctions when a large body of its citizens, as represented in Congress or by the president, conclude that some other nation's behavior is so egregious as to preclude normal economic relations. It is a fact that this point is reached rather sooner here than in most other countries, including other democracies. The French and the Japanese, for example, take a less idealistic (they would argue, less moralistic) view of their role in the world and do not like to let ideology get mixed up with commerce. For reasons that have spawned a thousand books, Americans have a different view of their nation and its foreign policy. The view that foreign relations need not reflect moral judgments is not popular here. While learned treatises and distinguished diplomats have long argued that international financial institutions, international commerce, and even our bilateral relations should not be "held hostage" to moralizing over human rights, most Americans seem to think that to carry on normal political and economic relations with oppressive regimes is distasteful and demoralizing. Congress repeatedly votes to stop such relations regardless of what our friends and allies are doing.

To argue against all unilateral sanctions, then, is to argue for subordinating America's moral judgments to an international lowest-common-denominator. It is to argue that we must wait for an international consensus that is . . . extremely rare. . . .

There is a second and deeper flaw in the argument against unilateral sanctions. It overlooks the unique position in the world now held by the United States, and underestimates the necessity of American leadership to the peace and prosperity we currently enjoy. The argument against sanctions would be far more powerful—though still not irrefutable—if it were made in Belgium or Holland. In a speech in October 1997, Secretary of State Madeleine Albright told students at Catholic University that "for almost as many years as I have been alive, the United States has played the leading role within the international system; not as sole arbiter of right and wrong, for that is a responsibility widely shared, but as pathfinder—as the nation able to show the way when others cannot." Is it possible that we must show the way with words and weapons, but refuse a leadership role when commercial advantage may be lost?

The history of this century is largely a story of progress when the United States led the international community—or, perhaps more accurately, through its leadership created an international community—and of disaster when we abandoned that role. This has been true of major security successes ranging from the creation of the League of Nations to the victory over Japan and Germany to the winning of the Cold War. It was equally true of the formation of the international financial system after World War II.

BRIBERY OF FOREIGN OFFICIALS

Consider an example of American leadership that is directly relevant to the sanctions case. Bribery of foreign government officials has been a common practice, especially in the Third World, when foreign investors sought favors from poorly paid officials who were supervising government contracting or privatization programs. From the viewpoint of the honest American business-man, there were two logical solutions: All foreign businessmen should stop using bribery or all should be permitted to do so. What businessmen feared was a situation in which Americans were forbidden to use bribery but their competitors were free to do so.

THE EFFORT TO CRIMINALIZE BRIBERY

Yet that is precisely the system Congress imposed in 1977, when it adopted the Foreign Corrupt Practices Act in response to the Watergate special prosecutor's discovery of bribery pay-ments to foreign officials by American corporations. Congress made the bribery of foreign officials a federal crime, rejecting the notion that competitive business advantage required—and justified—such conduct. Bribery was wrong, the law said, re-gardless of whether the French and the Japanese and the Ger-mans did it. American businessmen complained, and no doubt lost some business. But the American example was not without effect. There began a campaign of official U.S. pressure on both "briber" and "bribee" governments: the former to join us in making bribery of foreign officials a crime, and the latter to po-lice their officials better. This campaign was conducted directly in foreign capitals, through private organizations like Trans-parency International, and in multilateral organizations such as the Inter-American Development Bank and the Organization for Economic Cooperation and Development (OECD).

That campaign, fueled by American leadership, is having re-sults. In November 1997, the OECD's 29 member states—virtu-ally all the world's developed economies—plus Argentina, Brazil, and Chile adopted the Convention on Combating Bribery of Foreign Public Officials in International Business Transactions. In the last several years, country after country has criminalized bribery of foreign officials and ended the tax deductibility of what had once been considered a normal business expense. In-ternational conferences about corruption are frequent, and the issue is high on the agenda of most multilateral institutions. Progress is visible. Calls for repeal of the Foreign Corrupt Prac-tices Act, once common, are now rare. The business community has come to realize that the proper way to level the playing field is to raise the business practices of our competitors to our level, not to descend to theirs.

But this lesson has not been applied to the sanctions issue, where American companies pressure Congress for permission to emulate the amoral policies of their competitors. This might be a reasonable policy—for Belgium, or Switzerland, or Portugal. It is not a reasonable policy for the United States. The argument against unilateral sanctions is an argument against American leadership and suggests that if we cannot get some sort of majority vote from other traders and investors, we must set our scruples aside. Now, it would be one thing to argue that in the context of war unilateral American action is unwise because it might prove too costly. Take the Persian Gulf conflict of 1991: One could have argued—many people did—that if the United States were unable to assemble a coalition, it should not try to force Iraq out of Kuwait, because American casualties would be too high. In fact, a solo American effort would have been feasible and would have cost few casualties. But such an argument has moral weight because, in the context of war, the price we pay for world leadership may be measured in blood.

MORAL PRINCIPLES AT STAKE

In the sanctions context, the argument against unilateral action is far less weighty because only money is at stake. On one side of the equation are the profits of various corporations and their shareholders and, no doubt, the jobs of some Americans. On the other side there are important moral principles and sometimes vital security interests. Sanctions against Myanmar reflect civilized outrage at the murderous activities of its rulers. Sanctions against China, Iran, Iraq, and Libya reflect not only moral disapproval but also a sensible estimate of how their actions affect our national security.

In the case of China, it can be persuasively argued that our refusal to apply sanctions when China sold missiles and nuclear technology to Pakistan and other countries is what led India to conduct its nuclear tests, which in turn led to the Pakistani tests and considerable heightening of tension on the Subcontinent. The issue is whether foreign policy should be driven by commercial objectives or only informed by them. With China, the commercial stakes may be high, but the security stakes are higher still. . . .

AMERICAN LEADERSHIP

For the business of America at the close of the twentieth century is not business; it is leadership, in the search for security and peace as well as for prosperity. Successful leadership requires prudence in strategy and tactics and in the use of resources. Isolating China or any other country that runs afoul of legislation regarding such matters as human-rights abuses and arms sales is not a policy. It is at best a *tool* of policy, and like most tools it will sometimes be useful and sometimes not. The more basic issue is whether the United States will be able to pursue its own foreign policies—including its policies of promoting human rights and democracy, and combating nuclear proliferation and missile sales—with all the available tools. If we must wait for the consent of all other trading nations before employing economic sanctions as a policy tool, or must refrain from using sanctions whenever the short-term interest of an American exporter is harmed, that tool has in effect been discarded. We are then left with only one choice, words or war.

The corporate campaign against economic sanctions marshals many cogent arguments. But we must be clear: Leadership in the search for peace and in support of human rights is not the same thing as engagement through commerce. Leadership imposes costs, and Americans have reluctantly but determinedly paid them throughout this century. Perhaps in the twenty-first century we will refuse to do so; perhaps, with a century of wars behind us, we now seek only profit. If so, if we now choose doing business over leading the world, let us at least be honest about it. Let us not delude ourselves with propaganda about a "political engagement" whose success is measured in sales rather than in security or peace.

| *"As a substitute for military force . . . sanctions seldom achieve the desired change in the conduct of foreign countries."*

ECONOMIC SANCTIONS ARE INEFFECTIVE AT MAINTAINING PEACE

Gary Hufbauer

Sanctions are a foreign policy tool used to punish or persuade another country to change its behavior by restricting its ability to trade or cutting off its economic aid. In the following viewpoint, Gary Hufbauer argues that while imposing sanctions may occasionally achieve a particular foreign policy objective, sanctions generally make matters worse for innocent people and businesses. Furthermore, he maintains, sanctions imposed by the West rarely have an impact on authoritarian governments, who see them as an isolated measure that is unlikely to be followed by any display of force. Hufbauer holds the Maurice R. Greenberg Chair, director of studies, at the Council on Foreign Relations in New York. He is the coauthor of *Economic Sanctions Reconsidered*.

As you read, consider the following questions:

1. According to Hufbauer, what percentage of the world's population is affected by sanctions imposed by the United States?
2. Why were economic sanctions against South Africa the exception to the rule in achieving the desired result, in the author's opinion?
3. How does the liberal application of sanctions erode U.S. leadership, in Hufbauer's view?

Reprinted from Gary Hufbauer, "Foreign Policy on the Cheap," *The Washington Post National Weekly Edition*, Commentary, July 20–27, 1998, by permission of the author.

Stating the obvious, President Bill Clinton recently lamented that the United States has become "sanctions happy." Clinton, of course, is the same president who has signed laws for new punitive measures against India, Pakistan, Cuba, Iran and Libya and has used his executive powers to add to the rich legacy of sanctions inherited from past occupants of the White House.

No country in the world has employed sanctions as often as the United States has. The American infatuation with economic sanctions was sparked by President Woodrow Wilson when he was trying to sell the idea of the League of Nations to his countrymen, together with its newly crafted economic weaponry. Wilson famously declared in 1919: "A nation boycotted is a nation that is in sight of surrender. Apply this economic, peaceful, silent, deadly remedy and there will be no need for force. It is a terrible remedy." America didn't buy the League—the Senate refused to ratify U.S. membership in that precursor to the United Nations—but as the decades rolled on, America adopted Wilson's idea of sanctions as a diplomatic tool.

During the twentieth century, the United States has imposed economic sanctions more than 110 times. Economic sanctions entail the denial of customary export, import or financial relations with a target country in an effort to change the country's laws or policies. For example, the United States may block World Bank or International Monetary Fund loans in an effort to stem nuclear proliferation (India and Pakistan); or it may restrict trade with a country to change its human rights policies (Argentina, Chile and China). The current inventory of U.S. sanctions covers 26 target countries, accounting for over half of the world's population. Since the demise of the Soviet Union, Congress has felt freer to interfere in foreign policy, instructing the president on the minute details of imposing and waiving sanctions. In short, whenever tensions rise, sanctions become the favorite tonic of American diplomacy.

LESSONS LEARNED

What have we learned from this grand experiment in the diplomatic laboratory? Quite a lot.

First, as a substitute for military force—the Wilsonian notion—sanctions seldom achieve the desired change in the conduct of foreign countries. In plain language: Wilson was wrong. Perhaps one episode in five results in discernible changes abroad that can be traced to sanctions. The most recent qualified success was the election of Andres Pastrana as president of Colombia, following several years of U.S. sanctions directed personally against his predecessor, Ernesto Samper. Charging that Samper had accepted $6 million from the Cali drug cartel for his 1994 presidential campaign, the United States disqualified Colombia as a recipient of U.S. aid and took the unusual step of revoking Samper's entry visa, in effect declaring him *persona non grata*. These steps were, of course, not the only reason for Pastrana's victory, and probably not the major reason, but they were a contributing factor. Against this qualified success must be listed many unqualified failures: Haiti, Cuba, Libya, Iran, Iraq and China, to name the most prominent.

SOUTH AFRICA

Advocates of sanctions offer South Africa as their favorite example. Economic sanctions were not the deciding factor, but they helped pressure F.W. de Klerk to concede power to Nelson Mandela in 1994. Why doesn't the South African experience translate to Burma, Sudan, India and other miscreants? One reason is that South African sanctions were multilateral, not just a U.S. initiative. Another reason is that, even under apartheid, South Africa was semi-democratic, and the white minority cared what the rest of the world thought.

In fact, this is one of the ironies: Democratic countries, where the elite cares what the rest of the world thinks, are far more susceptible to sanctions than authoritarian countries isolated from world opinion. The contrast between Sudan and South Africa, or between Cuba and Colombia, could not be sharper. An unintended consequence of financial sanctions against Pakistan, a weak but semi-democratic state, open to world opinion, is that the penalties may help topple the government of Prime Minister Nawaz Sharif—as Pakistan slips into deep economic depression—and pave the way for a truly authoritarian and fundamentalist regime.

NOT A SUBSTITUTE FOR FORCE

The second lesson from the diplomatic lab is that it is naive to think of sanctions as a substitute for force when dealing with authoritarian powers. Draconian sanctions made little difference to the policies of Manuel Antonio Noriega in Panama, Raoul Cedras in Haiti or Saddam Hussein in Iraq. Only the use of force changed the governments of Panama and Haiti, and pushed Iraq out of Kuwait. The threat of force tempered Hussein's resistance to U.N. arms inspections early in 1998. But far more often, when U.S. presidents impose sanctions, they see them as an isolated measure, not as part of an escalating "force curve"—a steady progression from diplomatic protest, to economic sanctions, to military intervention; at each step, the target country knows worse is yet to come. The result of treating sanctions as a disconnected policy measure is that the United States has acquired a well-deserved reputation for bluffing: If an authoritarian adversary can withstand sanctions, it need not fear a surprise attack.

A third lesson is that economic sanctions can inflict pain on innocent people while at the same time increasing the grip of the leaders we despise. When sanctions are applied broadside— as against Haiti, Cuba and Iraq—the hardest hit are the most vulnerable: the poor, the very young, the very old and the sick. Left unharmed, and often strengthened, are the real targets: the political, military and economic elites.

HARD AND FAST

A fourth lesson is that sanctions applied hard and fast are more likely to succeed (all other circumstances being equal) than sanctions applied soft and slow. But this lesson poses a dilemma. Hard sanctions usually require multilateral cooperation, if not from the U.N. Security Council, at least from the industrial democracies. While the United States may be the sole military superpower, it is not the only economic player. Without the cooperation of Canada, Western Europe and Japan, the United States alone cannot deny a target country key imports, critical markets or vital finance. So the prescription for hard sanctions—sanctions with both economic and moral effect—amounts to a caution against going it alone. On the other hand, multilateral cooperation takes time to arrange, and often is unachievable. Quick U.N. sanctions against Iraq in 1990 were a notable exception; more typical was the measured international response to India's recent nuclear weapons tests.

Another dilemma posed by the "hard and fast" lesson is that in circumstances where sanctions alone have the best chance of success—against societies that are semi-democratic and open to world opinion—it goes against the American spirit to pile on. Instead, we prefer to escalate sanctions slowly so as to give leaders of the target countries time to reconsider. This tactic also gives them time to take evasive measures.

So why not just muddle along with our sanctions policy? After all, in the view of many American officials, the United States has a special responsibility to deal with misdeeds in many places, ranging from religious persecution in Russia and China to despots in Cuba and Burma. But since military force is too costly and diplomacy is too feeble, why not apply economic sanctions as the global salve to problems abroad and consciences at home? Why not drink the marvelous tonic of foreign policy on the cheap?

Too High a Cost

The reason, again to quote President Wilson, if not in the sense he intended, is that sanctions are a "terrible remedy." Start with the domestic costs. Estimates made by Kimberly Elliott, Jeffrey Schott and myself indicate that economic sanctions in place today cost the United States some $20 billion in lost exports annually, depriving American workers of some 200,000 well-paid jobs. It would be one thing if these costs were compensated from the public purse, so that everyone shared the burden; it is quite another when the costs are concentrated episodically on individual American firms and communities.

An Ineffective Policy

Sanctions—even when comprehensive and enjoying almost universal international backing for nearly six months—failed to get Saddam Hussein to withdraw from Kuwait. In the end, it took Operation Desert Storm. Other sanctions have also fallen short. The Iranian regime continues to support terrorism, oppose the Middle East peace process, and press ahead with its nuclear weapons program. Fidel Castro is still in place atop a largely authoritarian political and economic system. India and Pakistan were not deterred from testing nuclear weapons by the threat of draconian penalties. Libya has refused to produce the two individuals accused of the destruction of Pan Am 103. Sanctions could not persuade Haiti's junta to honor the results of an election. Nor could they dissuade Serbia and others to call off their military aggression. And China continues to export sensitive technologies to selected countries and remains a society where human rights are violated.

Richard N. Haass, *Brookings Policy Brief* No. 34, June 1998.

Then consider the morality. U.S. economic sanctions, along with Fidel Castro's own mismanagement, have helped close the income gap between Haiti and Cuba—by driving Cuban living standards downward toward the desperate Haitian level. Speaking of Haiti, that blighted economy has yet to recover from penalties imposed by the first Clinton administration. The multitudinous poor in Iraq, Iran and Vietnam are that much more miserable thanks to prolonged sanctions. With a little resolve, we could also worsen the lives of Nigerians, Indonesians and Burmese. Pope John Paul II had a point when he said during his visit to Cuba in January 1998 that the effects of economic sanctions are "always deplorable, because they hurt the most needy"—in effect, that ordinary Cubans, not Castro and his inner circle, are paying the price. The same would happen in these other ill-governed countries.

Finally, the liberal application of sanctions to every cause and country badly erodes U.S. leadership. When the United States applies sanctions to half the world's people, and when it imposes secondary sanctions on allies and friends, it prompts a reaction against American hegemony. Sanctions against China have neither shaken the leadership nor hindered the country's drive for growth. Sanctions against India will have approximately the same lack of effect. And few secondary sanctions do more than irritate U.S. allies. (Americans, above all, should understand symbolic offenses. The British tea tax imposed no real economic hardship on colonial Boston. It did inspire a revolution against the greatest power of the day.)

THE HAMILTON-LUGAR BILL

Recovery from this love affair will require decisive steps by the White House and the Congress. Clinton appears ready to start the cure, but much more needs to be done. Passage of the sanctions reform bill, introduced in 1997 by Republican Sen. Richard Lugar of Indiana, Democratic Rep. Lee Hamilton of Indiana and Republican Rep. Phil Crane of Illinois, would be a useful next step. This bill seeks "to establish an effective framework for consideration by the legislative and executive branches of unilateral economic sanctions." It proposes several sensible guidelines when economic sanctions are considered, either by the president or Congress. [The bill has not passed as of August 1998.]

The procedural reforms include increased executive branch consultation with Congress, public hearings, a cost-benefit analysis, a preference for targeted and multilateral measures whenever possible, presidential waivers for all legislatively imposed sanctions and sanctity of contracts. If passed, Hamilton-Lugar would be a landmark law.

ADDITIONAL STEPS ARE NEEDED

But additional steps are still needed:

• The United States should rarely impose sanctions when it cannot get the support of its friends. This Hamilton-Lugar benchmark needs to become standard operating procedure. Ideally, the U.N. Security Council should support the sanctions. At a minimum, the North Atlantic Treaty Organization (NATO) or groups of like-minded states in Latin America, Asia or the Middle East should endorse the effort.

• We should realize that the huge inventory of sanctions now in place could have tremendous value as diplomatic carrots, if the president were able to withdraw them to reward good foreign behavior. For that, the president must have unfettered freedom to lift sanctions step by step. Hamilton-Lugar states that the president "should" have waiver authority when Congress enacts a new sanctions measure. The Justice Department needs to go further than that: It should challenge in court any sanctions legislation that does not contain a national interest waiver that the president can exercise. The Glenn Amendment, mandating sanctions against India and Pakistan for their nuclear explosions, would make an excellent test case. Mandatory legislation of this nature unconstitutionally infringes the president's power in the realm of foreign affairs.

• When dealing with authoritarian regimes, the president should direct sanctions at rulers, not the populace at large. Iraqis are not our enemies. Nor are Cubans. We can single out individuals and agencies that give offense or outrage. We can devise civil and criminal penalties, buttressed by bounties, so that their persons and property are at risk whenever they venture outside their own territory.

• Finally, when the president imposes comprehensive sanctions on an authoritarian regime, he should view those sanctions as a prelude to the exercise of military force, not as a substitute for force. Unless we are prepared to remove bad governments with military force, we have no business heaping prolonged punishment on innocent people.

PERIODICAL BIBLIOGRAPHY

The following articles have been selected to supplement the diverse views presented in this chapter. Addresses are provided for periodicals not indexed in the *Readers' Guide to Periodical Literature*, the *Alternative Press Index*, the *Social Sciences Index*, or the *Index to Legal Periodicals and Books*.

Ian Bremmer and Benjamin Gilman	"Q: Should Congress Drop Economic Sanctions that Prevent Trade with Iran?" *Insight*, July 20, 1998. Available from 3600 New York Ave. NE, Washington, DC 20002.
Kimberly Ann Elliott	"The Sanctions Glass: Half Full or Completely Empty?" *International Security*, Summer 1998.
Eugene Gholz, Daryl G. Press, and Harvey M. Sapolsky	"Come Home, America," *International Security*, Spring 1997.
Fred Hiatt	"Speak Loudly—Forget the Stick," *Washington Post National Weekly Edition*, June 29, 1998. Available from 1150 15th St. NW, Washington, DC 20071.
Fred C. Iklé	"U.S. Folly May Start Another Korean War," *Wall Street Journal*, October 12, 1998.
George Kenney	"U.S. Policy Snarls in Bosnia," *Mediterranean Quarterly*, Winter 1998. Available from Duke University Press, Box 90660, Durham, NC 27708-0660.
Robert A. Pape	"Why Economic Sanctions Still Do Not Work," *International Security*, Summer 1998.
Renée-Marie Croose Parry	"Titanic: A Parable for Our Planet?" *Human Quest*, May/June 1998. Available from 1074 23rd Ave. North, St. Petersburg, FL 33704.
Gideon G. Rose	"The Exit Strategy Delusion," *Foreign Affairs*, January/February 1998.
William Safire	"The Kosovo Dilemma," *New York Times*, June 18, 1998.
Nancy DeWolf Smith	"Afghanistan Needs U.S. Intervention," *Wall Street Journal*, August 31, 1998.
Michael Walzer	"Lone Ranger," *New Republic*, April 27, 1998.

CHAPTER 4

HOW CAN WAR BE PREVENTED?

CHAPTER PREFACE

Many of the wars fought in the second half of the twentieth century—in Israel, Turkey, Rwanda, Sudan, Angola, Chechnya, Bosnia, and Kosovo, for example—are ethnic conflicts involving groups of people who had, in most cases, lived peacefully side-by-side for years before their country erupted into violence. Throughout these periods of stability, however, tensions may be growing until some incident sparks civil war. Once ignited, ethnic hostilities may not cease until one side has "cleansed"—killed or removed—the other side from the shared territory.

Outside nations are usually reluctant to become involved in ethnic wars, rationalizing that it is an "internal" problem and not the concern of others. But occasionally, public outcry over the potential genocide of an entire population compels foreign governments to step in and try and make peace between the warring parties. Some conflicts are resolved by forcing the warring parties to share political power, by trying to persuade the ethnic groups to give up their ethnic identity and take on a national identity (such as Yugoslavian as opposed to Serbian), or by international decree that a foreign power should govern or police the warring nation.

However, some analysts maintain that the peace in these situations lasts only as long as the enforcers remain. According to Chaim Kaufmann, a professor of international relations at Lehigh University in Bethlehem, Pennsylvania, the only way to guarantee peace in countries ravaged by ethnic violence is to accede to the demands of the dominant ethnic population and separate the different groups into homogenous areas. He cites a survey of twenty-seven ethnic civil wars in which lasting peace was achieved in nineteen of the conflicts when the ethnic groups were partitioned and granted autonomy of the areas where they formed the majority population. Kaufmann contends that partitioning or separating the ethnic groups into "national homelands" makes each group feel secure against any threats by its enemies.

The partitioning of countries into ethnic enclaves is just one possibility of how peace can be achieved in war-ravaged countries. Preventing global wars, however, requires different tactics. The authors in the following chapter discuss various methods of averting war.

> "The design most favorable [for
> forestalling new threats in Europe]
> is a gradual expansion of NATO
> with no predetermined limit on
> membership."

EXPANDING NATO WILL ENSURE PEACE IN EUROPE

Joshua Muravchik

The North Atlantic Treaty Organization (NATO) was formed after World War II to defend its member countries against an attack by a nonmember country. Since then, NATO has expanded from its original twelve members to sixteen, and the United States has proposed adding three more. In the following viewpoint, Joshua Muravchik asserts that NATO, which has allowed for a strong American influence overseas, is responsible for more than 50 years of peace in Europe. He argues that the alliance must be allowed to change and expand to preserve NATO and ensure continuing peace. Muravchik is the author of *The Imperative of American Leadership* and *Exporting Democracy*.

As you read, consider the following questions:

1. How did NATO and the American presence increase security in Europe, in Muravchik's opinion?
2. According to the author, how does membership in NATO affect its member countries?
3. What is Muravchik's response to the argument that enlarging NATO will antagonize Russia?

Reprinted from Joshua Muravchik, "A Bigger NATO?" *The American Enterprise*, July/August 1997, by permission of *The American Enterprise*, a Washington, D.C.–based magazine of politics, business, and culture.

The North Atlantic Treaty Organization (NATO), many have said, is history's most successful alliance. But can it survive its success? NATO was formed for the specific purpose of countering Soviet imperialism, but the Soviet Union now rests in the dustbin of history. Why should NATO continue unless it can serve new purposes?

PEACE IN EUROPE

The fact is, the Soviet Union did not create instability and war in Europe; instability and war in Europe created the Soviet Union. Largely due to NATO, we have experienced 52 years without a war among the powers of Europe, the longest such respite since the birth of the modern world.

The key was the American presence in Europe. America offered a shield against Soviet expansion, but the NATO alliance and the American presence also reduced insecurity in other ways. For the most part, it ended the contest of all against all that had characterized European history. France and Germany and other combinations of states with histories of enmity no longer feared one another.

American influence, anchored in NATO, also counteracted three other sources of war: despotism, privation, and colonialism. America actively fostered democratization, market economics, and decolonization. But as Bosnia served to remind us, the end of the Cold War does not assure international peace. Either a new, post-Cold War security architecture will be fashioned or a precarious one will grow up willy-nilly. There is no way to foresee all new threats in Europe, but the best formula for forestalling or attenuating them is the same one that has worked so well for so long: America, democracy, capitalism, and non-imperialism. The design most favorable to these ends is a gradual expansion of NATO with no predetermined limit on membership.

A GROWING NATO

In 1997, Poland, Hungary, and the Czech Republic will join NATO. Nine more states have applied. Fifteen others have joined the Partnership for Peace, a framework for states that want to formalize cooperative relationships with NATO. PFP members are assisted in developing the training, command, and communications systems that will enable them to participate jointly with NATO members in a variety of missions, such as peacekeeping in Bosnia. Finally, a special consultative mechanism has been created between NATO and Russia. A parallel one with

Ukraine will establish a security relationship without giving Russia reason for fear.

This may sound like a Rube Goldberg machine, but great vehicles of statecraft need not look streamlined, so long as they are pointed in the right direction. Europe's security blueprint must remain a work-in-progress as post-Soviet polities take form.

MEMBERSHIP RESOLVES DISPUTES

Membership in NATO will have a powerful psychological impact on those admitted. It will signify acceptance into the club of free, secure, and prosperous states. This will strengthen democratic and free-market institutions. It will have a similar effect on those hoping to get in. NATO has set forth criteria for entry that include democracy, economic and political stability, and the absence of border or internal ethnic conflicts. These requirements have already had a salutary effect on the aspirants. For example, Hungary and Romania, and Hungary and Slovakia, have formally resolved longstanding disputes.

NATO's LEGACY

As I have said many times, if the West does not stabilize the East, the East will destabilize the West. If principles of democracy win in the East, the peace and stability of all Europe will be insured. And not only to Europe. So the North Atlantic Treaty Organization expansion should be perceived as a continuous process, in which the nations of Central and Eastern Europe mature toward the meaning, values and goals of the enlarged and revived alliance.

Vaclav Havel, New York Times, May 13, 1997.

But should American boys die for Budapest, Prague, or Gdansk? Actually, any scenario that put these places at risk would entail conflict of a magnitude that would almost surely embroil the United States anyway. The effect of NATO expansion is to make such a scenario vastly less likely.

ADAPTING TO THE NEW REALITIES

Won't NATO expansion also antagonize Russia? To a degree, yes, but this has already been softened by the newly agreed consultative mechanism and can be mitigated further by maintaining that Russia, too, is not excluded from eligibility if it comes to meet the membership criteria. Moreover, there may be a greater problem with Russia if NATO does not expand. The old NATO is by definition an instrument of the Cold War: Its sole purpose was defense against the Soviet Union, which must now mean against Russia. Only an evolving NATO, which means one whose composition is changing, can grow into something other than an anti-Russian alliance.

Most of the arguments against NATO expansion boil down to arguments against NATO's continued existence, even though NATO has given Europe the longest peace it has enjoyed perhaps ever. To discard it would be utter folly. But to preserve it we must allow it to grow and adapt to new realities.

> "NATO's expansion could well
> provoke the most serious crisis
> in Europe since the onset of World
> War II."

EXPANDING NATO WILL NOT
ENSURE PEACE IN EUROPE

Stanley Kober

The North Atlantic Treaty Organization (NATO) was formed in
1949 as a defensive alliance among the United States, Canada,
Iceland, and nine European countries against Soviet aggression.
In the following viewpoint, Stanley Kober argues that Russia
may feel threatened if three former Soviet satellite countries are
added to the alliance. If Russia feels its security is at risk, it may
take actions to defend itself, he asserts. Because NATO guarantees to protect members in the alliance, those actions could easily lead to a nuclear war with Russia, Kober maintains. Kober is
a research fellow in foreign policy at the Cato Institute, a public
policy think tank.

As you read, consider the following questions:

1. According to Alexander Lebed, as cited by Kober, how will
   Russia react to a NATO expansion that includes its former
   satellites?
2. In the author's opinion, why is the threat of nuclear
   escalation more likely if NATO is expanded?
3. How will Russia react if the Baltic states are invited to join
   NATO, according to the author?

Excerpted from Stanley Kober, "NATO Expansion and the Danger of a Second Cold War,"
Cato Foreign Policy Briefing, January 31, 1996. Endnotes in the original have been omitted in this reprint.
Reprinted by permission of the Cato Institute, Washington, D.C.

A far-reaching public and congressional debate on the North Atlantic Treaty Organization (NATO) expansion is overdue. A meaningful debate must begin with the recognition that the countries of Central and Eastern Europe [Poland, Hungary, and the Czech Republic] want to be admitted to NATO because they are afraid of Russia, and given developments in that country, their fears are not wholly unjustified. The issue is whether NATO expansion is the proper way of addressing their fears or whether it would make the situation worse. A proper answer to that question must address two issues.

First, how will NATO expansion affect Russia? Despite the assurances of the advocates of expansion, there can be no serious question that expansion would evoke a hostile reaction from Moscow. "NATO . . . is emerging as the defining foreign policy issue in Russia today," reports the [London] *Observer*. "Nothing else incites such anti-Western rhetoric from the politicians." Former general Alexander Lebed . . . maintains that NATO expansion would require the creation of a countervailing military bloc by Russia and the cancellation of conventional and nuclear arms agreements. "A similar precedent was created in Poland in 1939," he has said, equating NATO expansion into Poland with the threat posed to Russia by Hitler's occupation. "The price of that precedent was 50 million lives. We won't get away with only 50 million today."

Given that sort of reaction, verbal declarations of NATO support will not suffice to make good on the NATO guarantee, which leads to the second question: what will the United States—and it will be the United States, not its European allies—do to make good on that guarantee? Americans would have to ask, for example, how much they would be willing to spend on increased conventional forces.

A NUCLEAR TRIP WIRE

Perhaps more to the point, how much risk of nuclear escalation is the United States willing to assume? Despite the assurances of some defense experts that the requirements for nuclear deterrence in an expanded NATO will be "radically different and smaller than during the Cold War," the opposite is likely to be the case. "We deem the strategic nuclear forces as the most important guarantor for safeguarding the military security of Russia and its allies," Defense Minister Pavel Grachev wrote in 1993, hinting strongly that Russia would use its nuclear weapons first, if necessary. "The essence of containment may reside in a timely and adequate retaliatory reaction to the actions undertaken by an aggressor who is preparing to attack," he continued. "Steps of solving the problem depend upon a readiness to inflict a strike against a possible opponent at any time with a damage not acceptable for him."

That threat was made explicit by a Russian journalist with good Defense Ministry connections after NATO's study on enlargement was published in September 1995.

> Russia's future reaction to any attempt to deploy foreign troops near its borders (including such a move under the guise of conducting maneuvers) is quite predictable. It will be exactly the same as Washington's reaction in 1961 [sic], when our troops landed in Cuba. First there will be a blockade (if the geographic location of the future conflict zone allows this), then an ultimatum demanding an immediate troop withdrawal and, if the ultimatum is not complied with, a preventive strike that would deprive the adversary of offensive capabilities.

Given Russia's conventional military weakness relative to NATO, such a strike presumably would have to be nuclear. Perhaps such threats are a bluff and are not to be taken seriously, but those who would dismiss them out of hand should recall Henry Kissinger's warning of 1985:

> If it were not for nuclear weapons it is likely that there would have been a war between us and the Soviets. So it is almost certainly true that nuclear weapons have preserved the peace. It is also true that if we continue the strategy that has got us these 40 years of peace, that some catastrophe somewhere along the line is going to happen and therefore the big problem of our period is to build on this long period of peace we have a structure that is different from the preceding one.

SOWING THE SEEDS OF MISTRUST

Whatever else NATO expansion may signify, it is certainly not building a structure different from what existed before. "Why are you sowing the seeds of mistrust?" Yeltsin asked NATO members in December 1994, adding that Europe was in danger of plunging into "a cold peace." The Russian elections—and the subsequent replacement of Andrey Kozyrev with hardliner Yevgeny Primakov as foreign minister—are an urgent warning about the deterioration of the relationship between Russia and the West. At this delicate time, the United States and its NATO partners should be wary of doing anything that would make the situation worse, especially if they have no serious intentions of backing up their verbal commitments. Security is not guaranteed by mere pledges: If NATO is expanded, a new confrontation becomes institutionalized, and the United States will be pressured by its European allies (old and new) to shoulder the additional burdens and risks. In particular, we must recognize that NATO entails a commitment to escalate to nuclear war, and as Kissinger pointed out, our luck may not hold forever.

PLAYING WITH FIRE

Expanding NATO violates the wise principle enunciated by Winston Churchill: "In victory, magnanimity." Churchill was no softy, but he recognized the stupidity of grinding the face of a defeated foe in the dirt. Less than ten years ago, Russia still had superpower status. Currently, its economy is in free fall, its military is a shambles, the life expectancy of its male population is at a Third World level. Russia is no threat, is not capable of purposeful and serious military action. But if humiliated further and made desperate, it could be dangerous in the way that a wounded animal can be dangerous—and it still has an enormous arsenal of nuclear weapons. In such circumstances, providing extreme elements in Russia with a cause they can exploit is playing with fire.

Owen Harries, *American Enterprise*, July/August 1997.

We should not underestimate the danger of the current situation. "Maybe the Cold War was in fact the Cold Peace," muses Andrei Filipov, a foreign affairs expert in Russia's increasingly influential Communist Party. "Maybe what we have now is a Cold War." If Filipov is right, the original Cold War will have been mild compared with what lies ahead.

The emergence of an anti-Western Russian political leadership would obviously lead to an escalation of global tensions, and nowhere would that effect be more pronounced than in Europe. At the same time, it is important to recognize that Russia does not at present pose a credible conventional military threat to Western Europe, nor is it likely to for some time, given the condition of the Russian military and economy. Moreover, the major West European powers can do much to protect their own security if a new threat does emerge.

TAUNTING A BULL WITH A RED CAPE

The Central and East European countries have greater reason to worry about a resurgent Russia. The pertinent question, however, is whether NATO expansion would improve or worsen their security. At the moment, Russian armed forces have their hands full with Chechnya, Tajikistan, and a number of lesser problems on the federation's periphery. NATO expansion might have the perverse effect of diverting Russia's attention from those problems to the situation on its western border. "You shouldn't try to intimidate, to stick a fist under someone's nose and tell them to behave," General Lebed has warned with regard to NATO expansion. "It is a mistake to taunt a bull with a red cape."

An especially dangerous flashpoint is the Baltic region. Although Russia's armed forces are too weak to attack Western Europe, they could still overpower the tiny Baltic republics. Eitvydas Bajarunas, an official with Lithuania's Ministry of Foreign Affairs, worries that Russian pressure would increase on countries excluded from NATO expansion. He argues that countries with no immediate prospect of membership need some other type of commitment, such as associate member status. If NATO does not create such arrangements, Bajarunas warns, "enlargement will reduce and not improve security in Europe as a whole."

GUARANTEES MUST BE SUPPORTED

That is the inherent dilemma of NATO expansion. . . . Security guarantees are more than verbal declarations; they must be backed up with real forces and determination. That lesson is being ignored, and a major confrontation may be forming as a result. NATO diplomats are reportedly telling the Baltic republics that their applications for membership in the alliance are a guarantee against any possible new invasion by Russia. But that is exactly the opposite of what the Russians are saying. "If NATO agrees to admit the Baltic republics, Russian Federation Armed Forces will immediately be moved into Estonia, Latvia, and Lithuania," *Komsomolskaya Pravda* reported about a new Russian defense doctrine adopted in September 1995. "Any attempt by NATO to stop this will be viewed by Russia as the prelude to a world nuclear catastrophe."

If such Russian statements are not a bluff, NATO's expansion could well provoke the most serious crisis in Europe since the onset of World War II. The East European countries are understandably worried about political developments in Russia, but the prospect of NATO membership's providing them with reliable protection against Russian expansionism is a cruel and dangerous illusion.

> "The United States and the Soviet
> Union might well have gone to war
> at some point in the last 50 years
> had the specter of nuclear
> annihilation not hung over both
> countries."

AN ARSENAL OF NUCLEAR WEAPONS PREVENTS WAR

Charles Krauthammer

In the following viewpoint, Charles Krauthammer argues that countries with nuclear weapons are less likely to go to war because they realize that a war may lead to nuclear annihilation. However, Krauthammer maintains, countries with just a few nuclear weapons are at a higher risk of nuclear war because it is much more tempting for a hostile nation to try and destroy all its enemy's nuclear weapons in a first strike. For that reason, he asserts, it is better for countries to have many nuclear weapons to reduce the possibility that these warheads will all be destroyed in a preemptive nuclear attack. Krauthammer is a syndicated columnist.

As you read, consider the following questions:

1. According to Krauthammer, what was the most stabilizing factor in the nuclear equation between the United States and Russia?
2. What should be the purpose of nuclear arms reduction agreements, in the author's opinion?
3. In Krauthammer's view, why is the total denuclearization of the United States a "crazy" idea?

Reprinted from Charles Krauthammer, "Thinking the Unthinkable . . . Again," *The Weekly Standard*, June 22, 1998, by permission of the author.

O ne of the least lamented casualties of the Soviet Union's demise was the arcane specialty of nuclear doctrine. Those who had wasted their youth studying the ins and outs of nuclear deterrence—the peculiar logic of nuclear war and the kinds of policies and weapons that might make it more or less likely—went the way of the blacksmith in the age of Henry Ford. Their skill was like conversational Latin: Its time had come and gone.

INDIA AND PAKISTAN

Or so it seemed. Now, thanks to India and Pakistan, deterrence theory is back. And it is needed. Every newspaper and commentator in the country is saying gravely that now that India and Pakistan have acquired nuclear weapons, the subcontinent is an area of great instability. What exactly does that mean?

After all, India and Pakistan have been at each other's throats for 50 years. They fought three wars. They routinely exchange rifle and artillery fire in Kashmir. Yes, the situation is more dangerous today. The stakes are obviously higher. Any war could be fought not just with conventional weapons but nuclear ones. But that does not necessarily mean that the subcontinent is more unstable.

Indeed, nuclear weapons can actually be stabilizing. The United States and the Soviet Union might well have gone to war at some point in the last 50 years had the specter of nuclear annihilation not hung over both countries. In the same way, India and Pakistan might be *less* likely to go to war if that means not just the loss of a few soldiers on the frontier, but the possible annihilation of one's major cities. This is true, however, only over the long run. In the short run, the nukes *are* destabilizing—but not for the reasons being advanced in the papers.

MORE IS BETTER

The subcontinent in the near term will be an area of great instability not just because, obviously, Pakistan and India are new at the nuclear game and thus will be prone to miscalculation, but because *each side has so few nuclear weapons*. This sounds odd. It is odd. But it reflects the central paradox of deterrence theory: Generally speaking, the more nukes the better. There is safety in numbers.

Now, conventional wisdom holds that the way to nuclear safety is to reduce numbers. That was the fuel for the frenzied nuclear disarmament movements of the early '80s and for the American obsession with arms control today. But conventional wisdom is wrong. When the numbers get very low, the nuclear balance becomes unstable.

Consider India and Pakistan. At the moment, each has a very small number of nuclear weapons and an equally small number of missiles on which those weapons might be delivered. In a time of crisis—say, fighting breaks out over Kashmir—this presents each side with the opportunity to destroy the other's entire nuclear arsenal in one fell swoop at the beginning of the conflict. Small numbers make for a small target. And a small target is a tempting target. It places a premium on preemption. It rewards striking first.

Conversely, each side fears that if it does not strike first, its nuclear arsenal could be wiped out in a first strike, leaving it naked to nuclear blackmail or to further nuclear attack. Because the side that destroys the other side's arsenal will have some of its nukes left over to intimidate the other's population. That intimidation could be enough to tip the scales of any war or even to induce the aggressed-against to a quick surrender. Very low numbers thus encourage a "use it or lose it" mentality. They promote the single most important contributor to nuclear instability: the temptation to preemption.

THE SECOND-STRIKE CAPACITY

Consider the U.S.-Soviet example. Apart from the few days of the Cuban missile crisis, the most unstable period was the late 1940s and early 1950s, when the United States and the Soviet Union were just developing their nuclear arsenals. There was even talk in Washington in the early '50s of destroying the Soviet arsenal before it could be developed. That kind of talk disappeared when the Soviets had built enough rockets, airplanes, and subs—enough redundancy—to make a first strike futile.

The essence of nuclear stability is the existence on both sides of a retaliatory or "second strike" capacity. If the other guy has such a capacity, it is crazy to launch a preemptive nuclear attack. No matter how massive or how accurate it is, it cannot succeed in wiping out all of his weapons. There would be enough left over for him to retaliate massively. A first strike would thus bring on the incineration of your own homeland. Result? You don't attack first. Nobody attacks first. And if nobody attacks first, there can be no nuclear war. QED.

That is how nuclear stability is established. Inconveniently for the doe-eyed arms controllers, this tends to happen at high levels of weaponry. More precisely, it is not the numbers that are decisive, but how they are distributed and how invulnerable they are to preemption. Thus the most stabilizing factor in the nuclear equation between the United States and the Soviet Union was the submarine forces. Their nuclear weapons could never be found with any accuracy by the enemy. They could thus never be preemptively destroyed. If either side were foolish enough to attack the other, there would always be the submarines to bring Armageddon on the aggressor. Huge, dispersed, mobile, and hardened arsenals of land-based and airborne nukes had the same stabilizing effect.

NUCLEAR WEAPONS ENHANCE SECURITY

It is often argued that nuclear weapons have no redeeming value, and that any state that goes nuclear is engaging in dangerous and self-defeating behavior. Thus, President Clinton maintains that India's recent nuclear tests were a "terrible mistake." The implication is that nuclear weapons should be eliminated altogether.

In fact, nuclear weapons are a superb deterrent for states that feel threatened by rival powers. Simply put, no state is likely to attack the homeland or vital interests of a nuclear-armed state for fear that such a move might trigger a horrific nuclear response. Not surprisingly, therefore, states are often tempted to acquire nuclear weapons to enhance their security.

John J. Mearsheimer, *New York Times*, May 17, 1998.

This explains why the nuclear-freeze hysteria of the early '80s was so pointless. It promoted not a panacea, not even a palliative, but a nullity. It also explains why the nuclear arms reduction agreements that so mesmerize the Clinton administration today are largely irrelevant. Yes, they are worth pursuing for their marginal economic savings and for reducing the stock of stuff that, if poorly tended, might be prone to accident or theft. These treaties do practically nothing, however, to enhance strategic stability.

Even worse is the movement today, led by such luminaries as Gen. Lee Butler, former head of the U.S. Strategic Air Command, to bring about (through gradual arms reduction) the total denuclearization of the United States. This idea, trumpeted for its boldness, is simply crazy.

THE GENIE IS OUT OF THE BOTTLE

Why? Because the nuclear genie is out of the bottle. There is no way to undo the knowledge of how to make the weapons. Many regimes can potentially make them. The only problem is acquiring the materials and the brains to assemble the devices. As Saddam Hussein has shown, a determined tyrant can do this under even the most stringent inspection regime. Remember: *Before* the Gulf War, Saddam was a card-carrying, paid-up, cooperating member of the Nuclear Non-Proliferation Treaty. He was regularly inspected by the International Atomic Energy Agency. And under the nose of that agency, he built not one but two clandestine nuclear programs. Were the United States to engage in the folly of total denuclearization, it would surely wake up one day looking down the barrel of some nuclear-armed bad actor—Iraq or North Korea or Iran or who knows what other rogue state of the future. Never in history would a Great Power have voluntarily put itself at such pointless risk.

After all, the ultimate instability—and vulnerability—occurs when one side has nukes and the other doesn't. Imagine what the world would have been like in the late 1940s if Stalin had acquired the bomb before we did. (Even worse, imagine if Hitler had.) Stalin might not have used the bomb. But the very fact that he *could* might have intimidated us into surrendering large parts of Europe, or even more.

The world was lucky that the first nuclear power was as benign a nation as the United States. It allowed us to go through the birth of the nuclear era in the most stable way: unilateral possession by a nonaggressive power. We used the bomb to end a war, not to start—or win by threat—new ones. Once the Soviets acquired theirs, however, a period of severe nuclear instability began.

Déjà Vu

That is where the India-Pakistan balance is now—about where we were in 1950. And it is U.S. policy today to try to rush in and get both sides to forswear the nukes: no further testing, no weaponization. This would be very nice. It is also very unlikely.

Indeed, it is likely that even if both sides agree, one side or the other will cheat. And it is certain that even if neither side does in fact cheat, both sides will surely suspect each other of doing just that. And when you suspect the other side of cheating, you suspect that it may have a first-strike capacity—which would spur you to cheat as well and develop a clandestine countervailing arsenal. Indeed, that is precisely what has happened between India and Pakistan—competing clandestine nuclear programs—to bring us to the current crisis.

The period of nuclear instability on the subcontinent is beginning. And paradoxically, the situation will only begin to sta-bilize when both countries have deployed enough nukes—spread out in enough areas—that neither side can be sure of a successful first strike. It sounds perverse to say it, but the fact is, now that the race is on, nuclear stability will only come to the Indian subcontinent when the respective nuclear arsenals have grown larger and more mature.

It is not a happy prospect. But it is reality. Welcome once again—just when you thought it was over—to the unthinkable world of nuclear deterrence.

"It has been asserted ... that nuclear
weapons help prevent war—but in
fact the five declared nuclear powers
have been involved in eight times as
many wars as the non-nuclear
countries since 1945."

AN ARSENAL OF NUCLEAR WEAPONS
WILL NOT PREVENT WAR

Dietrich Fischer

In the following viewpoint, Dietrich Fischer argues that the
world's entire arsenal of nuclear weapons should be destroyed.
Countries with nuclear weapons capabilities are more likely to
engage in war than countries without nuclear weapons, he contends. Furthermore, he asserts, it is only a matter of time until
hostile nations or terrorists will use nuclear weapons against
their enemies, which will lead to nuclear annihilation. Fischer is
a professor at Pace University in New York City and codirector
of TRANSCEND, an international network of scholars who work
to achieve peace in warring countries by peaceful means.

As you read, consider the following questions:

1. According to Fischer, why did India oppose the
   Comprehensive Nuclear Test Ban Treaty?
2. What percentage of American voters favors eliminating all or
   most nuclear weapons, according to a 1995 poll cited by the
   author?
3. How does Fischer respond to arguments that nuclear
   technology cannot be uninvented?

Reprinted from Dietrich Fischer, "Towards a Nuclear Weapons–Free World," Jinn,
November 19, 1996, by permission of Pacific News Service; © Pacific News Service.

Having won reelection, President Bill Clinton now aspires to leave a mark in history. The best way to do that is to help free humanity from the risk of a nuclear holocaust. This would be as significant an achievement as the abolition of slavery by Abraham Lincoln.

A WORLD FREE OF NUCLEAR WEAPONS

The year 1996 has brought us several steps closer to a world free of nuclear weapons. The World Court declared the threat or actual use of nuclear weapons contrary to international law. The Canberra Commission on the Abolition of Nuclear Weapons—which included former US Defense Secretary Robert McNamara and Gen. Lee Butler, former chief of the Strategic Air Command—proposed a concrete step-by-step plan to eliminate nuclear weapons in a verifiable way.

And on September 10, 1996, the Comprehensive Nuclear Test Ban Treaty was approved by the United Nations General Assembly by a vote of 158 to 3. (India opposed the treaty, purportedly because it set no date for the complete elimination of nuclear weapons.)

On signing the treaty, Clinton advocated further steps, including a ban on producing bomb-making materials, deeper cuts in nuclear weapons arsenals, improved verification, and stronger measures against smuggling of nuclear materials.

Clinton should go farther, and declare that the United States will never use nuclear weapons first, and invite other powers to begin work on a treaty eliminating all such weapons.

Clinton may face resistance from other members of the "nuclear club"—who think of themselves as occupying a privileged position—and from Republicans in Congress, who argue the Comprehensive Test Ban Treaty undermines American security.

In this case he can appeal directly to voters—82% favor eliminating all or most nuclear weapons, according to a 1995 poll. Similar treaties banning biological and chemical weapons already exist.

Why has an agreement to eliminate nuclear weapons eluded us? If Hitler had used nuclear weapons and lost the war, they would have been outlawed as cruel and inhuman long ago. But the fact that they were first used by the victorious side in a war considered just has given them an undeserved aura of legitimacy.

FLAWED ARGUMENTS

Over the last 50 years, many flawed arguments have been put forward to justify the policy of nuclear deterrence.

It has been asserted, for example, that nuclear weapons help prevent war—but in fact the five declared nuclear powers have been involved in eight times as many wars as the non-nuclear countries since 1945.

The claim that nuclear weapons have prevented nuclear war is preposterous. The threat of nuclear retaliation might deter a deliberate attack, but that is not the way every war begins. Rather, when tensions are high, events may escalate and it is sometimes hard to say who made the first move.

Countries with Nuclear Weapons Fight Wars

The favorite word in [the United Nations] presently is reform. It is very easy to say. However, to bring form to reform requires giving up old concepts, notions, attitudes and beliefs, of which the most classic is the belief that nuclear weapons can prevent war. Since the Second World War, we have seen several wars fought where, in some instances, even nuclear weapon-states were directly involved. Mercifully, nuclear weapons were not used.

Ahmed Mujuthaba, statement to the United Nations, October 23, 1997.

Relying on the threat of mutual destruction to deter war is like trying to prevent traffic accidents by packing your car with dynamite, putting a trip wire around it and telling everyone, "Don't hit me, or we will both die!" This should indeed stop people from hitting you intentionally, but any accidental collision would be fatal.

Russian Roulette

As long as the nuclear powers insist on the right to keep nuclear weapons, other countries, and ultimately terrorists, will want them, too. Once that happens, it is only a question of time until they are used, deliberately or by accident. We are playing Russian Roulette with our future.

We must reject playing the role of involuntary nuclear hostages. Nuclear weapons will not be abolished without a strong popular movement, just as the abolition of slavery, colonialism, and most recently apartheid came only after sustained public pressure.

There are those who admit we might be better off if nuclear weapons had never been invented, but argue they can not be uninvented—and therefore we have to live with them as long as civilization exists. But nobody has uninvented cannibalism. We simply abhor it. We can certainly learn to abhor the thought of incinerating entire cities with nuclear weapons.

"[War] is here to stay. . . . War is a consequence of original sin. In other words, war is part of the only human condition we can know. World peace is impossible because of the truths about human nature."

WAR CANNOT BE PREVENTED

Jeffrey Hart

In the following viewpoint, syndicated columnist Jeffrey Hart contends that the portrayals of war as consisting of glorious battles are inaccurate. War is full of pain, terror, and ugliness, he asserts. However, it is also exciting, giving an intensity to life that is not present in peacetime.

As you read, consider the following questions:

1. How does Steven Spielberg's depiction of war in *Saving Private Ryan* differ from most other war movies, in Hart's opinion?
2. How did soldiers in the time of Homer differ from modern soldiers, according to the author?
3. According to the historian cited by Hart, how many years of recorded human history have been free of wars?

Reprinted from Jeffrey Hart, "War Has Been with Us Since Adam and Eve," *Conservative Chronicle*, August 12, 1998, by permission of King Features Syndicate.

S teven Spielberg has done an audacious thing with his *Saving Private Ryan*, taking on one of the most profound subjects of artistic representation—war—and portraying not only its horrors but its deep mystery, its appeal and its hold upon us.

In the film's opening sequence, which lasts about 25 minutes, Spielberg presents a full frontal view of D-Day on Omaha Beach in 1944.

With few exceptions, war has been sanitized in the movies. Soldiers in most John Wayne movies, for example, die cleanly. They stagger, maybe utter a word or two and then die with a bullet through the heart.

But Spielberg rolls the artistic dice, and in his first 25 minutes gives us the assault as it really was, the full butcher shop, with limbs shattered, intestines in the water, heads blown away, soldiers dead before they could get out of the landing barge, soldiers too frightened to fire a single shot at the enemy. Terror. Panic. Chaos.

In those 25 minutes, Spielberg moves the visual representation of war to a new level.

War is such an extreme experience that representing it, talking about it, let alone justifying it, raises serious problems.

WAR IS HELL

It is well-known that Gen. William Tecumseh Sherman, one of the fiercest generals of all time, said war is hell. Actually, he said, "I am tired and sick of war. Its glory is all moonshine. It is only those who have neither fired a shot nor heard the shrieks and groans of the wounded who cry aloud for blood, more vengeance and more desolation. War is hell."

The great general certainly had a right to that opinion. But listen to his great contemporary, Oliver Wendell Holmes Jr., a veteran severely wounded three times in the Civil War, addressing the Harvard graduating class of 1895:

"War, when you are at it, is horrible and dull. It is only when time has passed that you see that its message was divine."

One of the things that such sensitive men as Ernest Hemingway apparently felt when they came back to America after World War I was disgust at the way the war was surrounded by lies, told by civilians and especially by officials. The notion that people such as Woodrow Wilson justified the slaughter as a war to end war disgusted such men, who knew that war is deeper than that.

Homer's Bronze Age warriors were raised from childhood to fight, and they did not value old age. They lived and died for valor and immortal fame. A modern soldier brought up with civilian expectations is in a different situation. Unlike Achilles, he has not been raised as a warrior. As he trains for battle, he needs to understand that death will be close at hand, that in combat one takes short views.

THE POWER OF WAR

For all their relative shortcomings, however, modern soldiers also touch the mystery of war.

Hemingway, for example, sometimes tried to express the slaughterhouse aspect of war directly, but more often he expressed it indirectly through its effect on those who had been in it, who were wounded psychologically, hollowed out, maybe driven mad.

Hemingway also discovered that soldiers live intensely because of the awareness of death—which is something Homer also knew.

Pontius' Puddle. Reprinted by permission of Joel Kauffmann.

Not many readers today are aware of the English poet Edmund Blunden, whose early fame rested on his powerful poems about the horrors of the Western Front during World War I. Blunden also knew what Hemingway discovered: that in war one can live with a special intensity.

Thus in Blunden's great poem 1916 Seen From 1921, he says he finds peace dull, that peace makes him feel prematurely old.

A representation of war that does not capture its double truth—that it is awful but also powerful and vital—is merely propaganda.

St. Augustine knew something else about war: that it is here to stay. He said war is a consequence of original sin. In other words, war is part of the only human condition we can know. World peace is impossible because of the truths about human nature.

A historian has calculated that there were 19 years in all of recorded history when there was no war going on somewhere.

TWO GREAT THEMES

Our first poem, The Iliad, is about war. So is the first Bible episode following the Fall, the murder of Abel by Cain, doubtless reflecting some war between growers and herders.

War is one of the two great themes of art and literature. Love is the other—which is why we have the two great poems there at the beginning, not only The Iliad but also The Odyssey.

You no doubt will decide for yourself how successfully Steven Spielberg deals with the complicated and omnipresent fact of war. However you judge that, we must applaud him for not being afraid to engage the deepest levels of human truth.

PERIODICAL BIBLIOGRAPHY

The following articles have been selected to supplement the diverse views presented in this chapter. Addresses are provided for periodicals not indexed in the *Readers' Guide to Periodical Literature*, the *Alternative Press Index*, the *Social Sciences Index*, or the *Index to Legal Periodicals and Books*.

Sebastian Barry	"Northern Ireland's War over Peace," *New York Times*, July 14, 1998.
James K. Boyce and Manuel Pastor Jr.	"Aid for Peace," *World Policy Journal*, Summer 1998.
Sam Cohen	"Save the Nukes," *National Review*, February 10, 1997.
Robin Fox	"Too Much Memory," *National Interest*, Winter 1997–98.
Iain Guest	"Ways That Warring Neighbors Can Live Together," *Christian Science Monitor*, December 19, 1996.
Owen Harries	"The Dangers of the Expansive Realism," *National Interest*, Winter 1997–98.
Issues and Controversies On File	"Northern Ireland's Future," December 26, 1997. Available from Facts On File, 11 Penn Plaza, New York, NY 10001-2006.
Chaim Kaufmann	"Possible and Impossible Solutions to Ethnic Civil Wars," *International Security*, Spring 1996.
James Kurth	"NATO Expansion and the Idea of the West," *Orbis*, Fall 1997.
Harvey Sicherman	"The Containment of America," *Orbis*, Summer 1998.
R. Jeffrey Smith	"A Believer No More," *Washington Post National Weekly Edition*, December 22-29, 1997. Available from 1150 15th St. NW, Washington, DC 20071.
Javier Solana and Melvyn Krauss	"Do We Need New Allies?" *Wall Street Journal*, March 12, 1998.
Margaret Thatcher	"The Present Danger," *Hoover Digest*, Winter 1998. Available from Hoover Press, Stanford University, Stanford, CA 94305-6010.

APPENDIX: GLOBAL CONFLICTS BY WORLD REGION

The following is a survey of global conflicts and their status as of October 1998.

Africa

Democratic Republic of Congo—In a bloodless May 1997 coup, rebels led by Laurent Kabila overthrew Mobutu Sese Seko—the dictator of Congo (the former Zaire) for 32 years. But after failing to keep his campaign promises, Kabila himself became the target of a revolt. The governments of Rwanda and Uganda which had supported Kabila's coup decided in 1998 to support the rebels seeking to oust him. At the same time Angola and Zimbabwe, which have a financial stake in Kabila's government, entered the civil war in support of Kabila.

Rwanda/Uganda—Rwanda is the home of two main ethnic groups—the majority Hutus and the minority Tutsis. Fighting in Rwanda between the Hutu-led government and the Tutsi-dominated Rwandese Patriotic Front (RPF) rebels first started in October 1990. In February 1993 the governments of Rwanda and neighboring Uganda, where RPF rebels had established camps, requested UN intervention following the failure of a number of cease-fires negotiated by the Organization of African Unity. Approximately 2,600 UN troops were sent to Rwanda in 1993 after the signing of the Arusha Peace Agreement that promised elections. On April 6, 1994, the Hutu president of Rwanda, Juvenal Habyarimana, was killed in a plane crash. Government soldiers, suspicious about the crash, started a new round of fighting that included the slaughter of 500,000 civilians, mostly Tutsis and moderate Hutus and resulted in a mass exodus of refugees to neighboring countries. Following the deaths of ten Belgian peacekeepers, all but 270 UN troops were withdrawn from the country. After four months of fighting, the RPF rebels succeeded in overthrowing the government and ending the major fighting. Fearing that hostilities would erupt again, the refugees lived in refugee camps in Uganda and Zaire until 1996, when they were forced by the host governments to return to their homes. The civilians' fears seem justified as Hutu militias and Tutsi soldiers continue a guerrilla war in the Rwandan countryside.

Somalia—In 1991, the United Somali Congress, an ethnic, clan-based rebel faction led by Mohammed Farah Aidid, succeeded in overthrowing the military dictatorship of Mohammed Siad Barre, who had ruled Somalia since 1969. Following the coup, a civil war between Aidid's forces and other factions who had opposed Siad Barre quickly ensued. In April 1992, 3,000 UN troops began a humanitarian operation to bring relief supplies to victims of a famine caused by the civil war. Because humanitarian efforts were blocked by the factions, the United

States sent more than 27,000 military personnel in December 1992 to protect the relief supplies. In May 1993, in the face of growing violence in Somalia, the United Nations took the unprecedented step of authorizing and using force to protect the relief supplies. The UN also changed the focus of its mission from providing humanitarian aid to apprehending Aidid, a mission that ultimately proved to be unsuccessful. In October 1993, a company of U.S. Rangers were surrounded by Somali militiamen, and eighteen Americans were killed. A public outcry by Americans against the deaths led to a withdrawal of the U.S. forces from Somalia; the American troops were replaced by those of other countries in March 1994.

Americas

Haiti—In September 1991, the Haitian military overthrew Haiti's first democratically elected president, Jean-Bertrand Aristide. With the failure of efforts to negotiate a political settlement to reinstate Aristide, the United Nations imposed economic sanctions on Haiti in December 1993. The United States succeeded in brokering the July 1993 Governor's Island Accord between Aristide and the Haitian military, ensuring Aristide's return to the presidency. The accord was broken in October 1993, however, when U.S. troops, who were to oversee Aristide's reinstatement, were blocked from landing in Haiti. In response, the United Nations imposed stronger sanctions on Haiti. UN human rights observers sent in September 1993 were expelled by the Haitian military in July 1994. The UN then authorized the use of force to restore democracy in Haiti, and a U.S.-led coalition of forces began preparing to invade. On September 18, 1994, the military junta agreed to step down and uphold the Governor's Island agreement, and U.S. military forces that had been poised to invade Haiti instead entered the country peacefully to ensure the transfer of power. However, Haiti has been without a government since June 1997 following allegations of fraud during the presidential election. About 500 U.S. troops remain in Haiti to build schools and bridges and to offer medical treatment to Haitians.

Asia

India/Pakistan—India and Pakistan have been fighting for control of the border area of Kashmir since both countries gained independence in August 1947. The United Nations first sent peacekeepers in January 1949 to observe a cease-fire that in July 1949 became a formal peace agreement. In 1971–1972 the peace agreement was broken and a new cease-fire was established. Hostilities in the form of threats and minor armed clashes between the two countries continue, and tensions have heightened since May 1998, when India exploded a nuclear bomb and Pakistan responded by detonating its own bomb two weeks later.

Afghanistan—In 1979 the Soviet Union invaded and occupied Afghanistan to support the communist regime that took power in 1978. U.S.-sponsored Afghan guerrillas drove out the communists in 1992, but factional fighting has engulfed the country ever since. Since 1996, the Islamic fundamentalist group known as the Taliban has gradually captured towns and villages in most of the country in its efforts to impose its strict interpretation of Islamic rule. Afghanistan's neighbors, especially Iran and the former Soviet republics of Tajikistan, Turkmenistan, and Uzbekistan, are nervous over the Taliban's expansion, fearing an influx of refugees and weapons. The first major battle between Iran and Afghanistan was reported in October 1998, perhaps as retaliation for the capture and killing of ten Iranian diplomats and one Iranian journalist by the Taliban in August 1998. More than 1.5 million Afghanis have died since the 1980s.

Europe

Chechnya—Following the collapse of the Union of Soviet Socialist Republics in 1991, the republics of the union individually declared their independence. Most of the republics were autonomous and were able to establish their independence peacefully. However, Russian president Boris Yeltsin refused to recognize the claims of autonomy and independence of Chechnya, a small, ethnic enclave on the border of the Russia and Georgia republics that had been only semiautonomous in the Russian federation. After numerous peace talks broke down, Yeltsin ordered Russian troops into the area in late 1994 and the rebellion was quashed.

Kosovo—The 2 million inhabitants of the Serb-ruled province of Kosovo are 90 percent ethnic Albanians, known as Kosovars. Kosovo was a semiautonomous province of Yugoslavia until 1989, when Yugoslavian president Slobodan Milosevic revoked the country's autonomy. The Kosovo Liberation Army (KLA) and ethnic Albanian leader Ibrahim Rugova are now insisting on full independence. Since March 1998, when the Serb army began a violent crackdown on the KLA, approximately 250,000 ethnic Albanians have been driven from their homes. Afraid that a war between the Serbs and Kosovars would escalate to include Albania, Macedonia, and Greece, the North Atlantic Treaty Organization demanded in October 1998 that Milosevic withdraw his troops from Kosovo or else Serbian bases would be subject to air strikes by NATO forces. Milosevic was also forced to pledge to restore self-government to Kosovo, to hold elections in Kosovo by July 1999, and to allow international observers to verify compliance with the NATO demands.

Northern Ireland—The Irish have been fighting for their independence since the fourth century when the Romans conquered the British Isles. In the twelfth century, Pope Adrian IV gave Ireland to the English king Henry II. The Protestant English, who began colonizing northern Ireland in the 1600s, gradually became the ruling class in Ireland, and the Irish Catholics became a minority in northern provinces of the country. The Irish Republican Army (IRA) was formed in 1857 to fight for independence from British rule. In 1916, Irish "home rule" advocates staged a dramatic, though small, Easter Rebellion. The British crushed the rebellion and jailed several of its leaders. Fearing widespread violence, the English organized a treaty in 1921 that separated Ireland into the Irish Free State in the south and the British-ruled counties in the north. A civil war broke out in the 1960s between those who supported the treaty (unionists) and those who wanted a united Ireland (nationalists). A peace agreement in April 1998 between Sinn Fein, the political arm of the IRA, and the British led to the election of a new assembly comprised of both parties in May 1998.

Former Yugoslavia—In June 1991, the republics of Slovenia, Croatia, and Macedonia declared independence from Yugoslavia. A war between the breakaway Croatia and what was left of the federal Yugoslav government in the Serbian republic was settled by a cease-fire brokered by the United Nations in January 1992. Following that settlement, Bosnia-Herzegovina declared its independence, precipitating a civil war among the Serb, Croat, and Muslim groups of that republic. Worsening the situation, both Croatia and Serbia have been accused of sending their armed forces to fight in Bosnia, and all sides in the conflict have been accused of "ethnic cleansing"—the use of rape, murder, terror, and concentration camps to force the evacuation of particular ethnic groups from certain areas. In March 1992 the United Nations sent 22,000 peacekeepers to the former Yugoslavia to prevent Serbian aggression against Macedonia, to protect civilians and humanitarian relief supplies in Bosnia, and to observe the cease-fire between Croatia and the federal government. In February 1994 the United Nations took the unprecedented step of authorizing North Atlantic Treaty Organization forces to conduct air strikes against the Serbs for their continued aggression. In December 1995, the Dayton Accords peace agreement was signed, giving 51 percent of Bosnia to the Muslim-Croat federation and 49 percent to the Serbs. Western allies were to provide 60,000 troops to oversee the cease-fire.

Middle East

Iraq/Kuwait—In August 1990, Iraq invaded neighboring Kuwait and attempted to annex it. In response, the United Nations approved the use of force to remove Iraq's army from Kuwait, and in January-February 1991 a U.S.-led multinational force defeated Iraq's military and liberated Kuwait. To safeguard against further aggression, UN troops were deployed to a demilitarized zone along the Iraq/Kuwait border established in April 1991. Further, in accordance with UN resolutions, UN inspectors are monitoring the dismantling of Iraq's nuclear and chemical weapons manufacturing capabilities. Also, the United States and its Gulf War allies are enforcing a ban on Iraqi military flights over the nation's Kurd-inhabited north and Shiite-dominated southern regions. The flight ban is a continuation of Operation Provide Comfort begun in April 1991, which disburses humanitarian aid to Iraqi Kurds, who were victims of governmental aggression before and after the Gulf War.

Israel/Palestine—War quickly broke out between Israel and its Arab neighbors following Israel's declaration of statehood in May 1948. After years of sporadic fighting with Syria, Jordan, and Egypt, Israel began to make peace with its neighbors during the late 1970s. In 1987, Palestinians living in Israel began a rebellion—known as the *intifada*—against Israeli rule. Secret talks in Oslo in 1991 and 1993 led to a peace agreement between the Israelis and Palestinians. Israel withdrew troops from portions of Gaza, Jericho, and the West Bank, which were then to be ruled by former Palestinian Liberation Organization leader Yasser Arafat. However, peace prospects in Israel remain shaky due to sporadic acts of terrorism by those who are opposed to the peace process.

Lebanon—In 1975, various Christian and Muslim militias in Lebanon began a civil war that left the country without a government for over fifteen years. In 1978, a UN peacekeeping force was sent to separate the militias and work to restore government. However, when 241 U.S. Marines were killed in a terrorist attack in October 1983, and many other European soldiers were killed in similar attacks, the forces were withdrawn. Since 1991, a new government in Lebanon has successfully worked to restore order and defeat or disarm the militias. However, attacks on Israel from terrorists based in Lebanon led to an Israeli invasion in 1978 and control of a nine-mile-wide "security zone" in southern Lebanon along their shared border. Israel continues to direct military action against targets in this "security zone."

FOR FURTHER DISCUSSION

CHAPTER 1

1. Melanie McDonagh maintains that wars are fought because of decisions made by political leaders. Ken Coates argues that impoverished nations have unstable governments and are therefore at a higher risk for fighting wars. David A. Lake and Donald Rothchild contend that one group will attack another group out of fear for its security. How does Matthew Parris respond to these arguments? Which viewpoint do you think is strongest? Explain your answer.

2. This chapter examines several alternatives for the causes of wars. Can you think of other explanations that were not included in this chapter? Give examples of wars that were fought for those reasons.

CHAPTER 2

1. Lionel Rosenblatt and Larry Thompson argue that a standing international army sponsored by the United Nations is necessary to maintain peace in small, intrastate wars. Do you think their proposal is a viable option for maintaining peace? Why or why not?

2. Joseph R. Rudolph Jr. cites numerous problems with peacekeeping interventions. Do you agree with his concerns? Why or why not?

3. Michael Parenti argues that U.S. humanitarian intervention is frequently a pretext for hidden political agendas that end up helping the oppressors rather than the oppressed. What is Shridath's Ramphal's solution to this situation? Do you agree with Ramphal's assertion that the international community has a moral obligation to intervene in another country's affairs? Why or why not?

CHAPTER 3

1. Andrew Bard Schmookler, Patrick J. Buchanan, John Hillen, and Stephen J. Solarz and Michael E. O'Hanlon argue over the role of the United States as the world's police force. Based on your readings of the viewpoints in this book, should the United States intervene in regional conflicts? If so, what should be the criteria required for intervention? Support your answer with examples from the viewpoints.

2. Elliott Abrams contends that sanctions are a necessary and effective way to persuade a nation's leaders to change their poli-

cies. Gary Hufbauer asserts that sanctions are effective only in harming innocent people and businesses. Which author makes a stronger case? Explain your answer.

CHAPTER 4

1. According to Stanley Kober, expanding the North Atlantic Treaty Organization (NATO) to include three former Soviet satellite countries will anger and threaten Russia, making prospects for peace in Europe less secure. How does Joshua Muravchik respond to Kober's concerns? Which viewpoint do you think is strongest? Explain your answer.

2. Charles Krauthammer argues that having a large number of nuclear weapons actually prevents a nuclear war because it is more difficult for the enemy to destroy all of the warheads at once. Dietrich Fischer contends, however, that that the claim that nuclear weapons have prevented nuclear war is preposterous. Based on your reading of the viewpoints, which argument is strongest? Support your answers with examples from the viewpoints.

ORGANIZATIONS TO CONTACT

The editors have compiled the following list of organizations concerned with the issues debated in this book. The descriptions are derived from materials provided by the organizations. All have publications or information available for interested readers. The list was compiled on the date of publication of the present volume; the information provided here may change. Be aware that many organizations take several weeks or longer to respond to inquiries, so allow as much time as possible.

Amnesty International USA
322 Eighth Ave., New York, NY 10001
(212) 807-8400 • fax: (212) 627-1451
website: http://www.amnesty-usa.org
http://www.amnesty.org/ailib

Amnesty International works to ensure that governments do not deny individuals their basic human rights as outlined in the United Nations Universal Declaration of Human Rights. It publishes numerous books, *The Amnesty International Newsletter*, *Country Reports* on individual countries, and an *Annual Report*.

Brookings Institution
1775 Massachusetts Ave. NW, Washington, DC 20036
(202) 797-6000 • fax: (202) 797-6004
e-mail: brookinfo@brook.edu • website: http://www.brook.edu

Founded in 1927, the institution conducts research and analyzes global events and their impact on the United States and U.S. foreign policy. It publishes the *Brookings Review* quarterly as well as numerous books and research papers on foreign policy.

CARE
151 Ellis St., Atlanta, GA 30303
(800) 521-CARE • (404) 681-2552
e-mail: info@care.org • website: http://www.care.org

CARE is the world's largest private, nonprofit, nonsectarian relief and development organization. It operates programs in disaster relief, food distribution, primary health care, agriculture and natural resource management, population, and small business support. It publishes the quarterly *CARE World Report* and occasional *CARE Briefs*.

Cato Institute
1000 Massachusetts Ave. NW, Washington, DC 20001-5403
(202) 842-0200 • fax: (202) 842-3490
website: http://www.cato.org

The institute is a libertarian public policy research foundation dedicated to peace and limited government intervention in foreign affairs. It publishes numerous reports and periodicals, including *Policy Analysis* and *Cato Policy Review*, both of which discuss U.S. policy in regional conflicts.

Center for Strategic and International Studies (CSIS)

1800 K St. NW, Washington, DC 20006
(202) 887-0200 • fax: (202) 775-3199
website: http://www.csis.org

CSIS is a public policy research institution that specializes in the areas of U.S. domestic and foreign policy, national security, and economic policy. The center analyzes world crisis situations and recommends U.S. military and defense policies. Its publications include the journal The Washington Quarterly, the monograph series The Washington Papers, and the reports Transnational Threats from the Middle East: Crying Wolf or Crying Havoc? and The Iraq Crisis: A Chronology of the "War of Sanctions."

Council on Foreign Relations

58 E. 68th St., New York, NY 10021
(212) 434-9400 • fax: (212) 986-2984
website: http://www.foreignrelations.org

The council specializes in foreign affairs and studies the international aspects of American political and economic policies and problems. Its journal Foreign Affairs, published five times a year, includes analyses of current ethnic conflicts around the world.

Foreign Policy Association (FPA)

470 Park Ave. South, 2nd Fl., New York, NY 10016
(212) 481-8100 • fax: (212) 481-9275
e-mail: info@fpa.org • website: http://www.fpa.org

FPA is a nonprofit organization that believes a concerned and informed public is the foundation for an effective foreign policy. Publications such as the annual Great Decisions briefing book and the quarterly Headline Series review U.S. foreign policy issues in China, the Persian Gulf and the Middle East, and Africa.

Global Exchange

2017 Mission, #303, San Francisco, CA 94110
(415) 255-7296 • fax: (415) 255-7498
e-mail: info@globalexchange.org
website: http://www.globalexchange.org

Global Exchange is a human rights organization that exposes economic and political injustice around the world. In response to such injustices, the organization supports education, activism, and a noninterventionist U.S. foreign policy. It publishes Global Exchanges quarterly.

Heritage Foundation

214 Massachusetts Ave. NE, Washington, DC 20002-4999
(800) 544-4843 • (202) 546-4400 • fax: (202) 544-6979
e-mail: pubs@heritage.org • website: http://www.heritage.org

The foundation is a public policy research institute that advocates limited government and the free-market system. The foundation publishes the quarterly Policy Review as well as monographs, books, and papers supporting U.S. noninterventionism.

Human Rights Watch
350 Fifth Ave., 34th Fl., New York, NY 10118-3299
(212) 290-4700 • (212) 736-1300
website: http://www.hrw.org

Founded in 1978, this nongovernmental organization conducts systematic investigations of human rights abuses in countries around the world. It publishes many books and reports on specific countries, including *Africa Watch*, *Americas Watch*, *Asia Watch*, *Helsinki Watch*, and *Middle East Watch*; and *The Human Rights Watch Quarterly*.

Institute for Policy Studies
733 15th St. NW, #1020, Washington, DC 20005
(202) 234-9382 • fax: (202) 387-7915

This nonpartisan center for research and education sponsors critical examination of the assumptions and policies that define America's stance on domestic and international issues and offers alternative strategies. It publishes books, including *Global Focus: A New Foreign Policy Agenda 1997–1998*, as well as reports, guides, and policy papers on foreign policy and related issues.

Overseas Development Council (ODC)
1875 Connecticut Ave. NW, Suite 1012, Washington, DC 20009
(202) 234-8701 • fax: (202) 745-0067
website: http://www.odc.org

The council is a public policy research institution that focuses on global issues such as poverty and economic and political development. ODC provides analysis, information, and evaluation of multilateral policies and actions. It publishes *Policy Focus* seven to ten times per year and *U.S.-Third World Policy Perspective* quarterly.

Reason Foundation
3415 S. Sepulveda Blvd., Suite 400, Los Angeles, CA 90034
(310) 391-2245 • fax: (310) 391-4395
website: http://www.reason.org

The foundation promotes individual freedoms and free-market principles, and opposes U.S. interventionism in foreign affairs. Its publications include the monthly *Reason* magazine.

Resource Center for Nonviolence
515 Broadway, Santa Cruz, CA 95060
(831) 423-1626 • fax: (831) 423-8716
e-mail: rcnv@rcnv.org • website: http://www.rcnv.org

The Resource Center for Nonviolence was founded in 1976 and promotes nonviolence as a force for personal and social change. The center provides speakers, workshops, leadership development, and nonviolence training programs and also publishes a newsletter, *Center Report*, twice a year.

Trilateral Commission
345 E. 46th St., New York, NY 10017
(212) 661-1180 • fax: (212) 949-7268
e-mail: trilat@panix.com • website: http://www.trilateral.org

The commission encourages shared leadership responsibilities among the countries in North America, Western Europe, and Japan. It publishes the annual magazine *Trialogue* and the report *Advancing Common Purposes in the Broad Middle East*.

United Nations Association of the United States of America
801 Second Ave., New York, NY 10017
(212) 907-1300
website: http://www.unausa.org

The association is a nonpartisan, nonprofit research organization dedicated to strengthening both the United Nations and U.S. participation in the council. Its publications include the bimonthly newspaper the *Interdependent*.

BIBLIOGRAPHY OF BOOKS

Elliott Abrams — *Security and Sacrifice: Isolation, Intervention, and American Foreign Policy.* Indianapolis: Hudson Institute, 1995.

Barbara Benton, ed. — *Soldiers for Peace: Fifty Years of United Nations Peacekeeping.* New York: Facts On File, 1996.

David Callahan — *Unwinnable Wars: American Power and Ethnic Conflict.* New York: Hill and Wang, 1998.

Tim Pat Coogan — *The Troubles: Ireland's Ordeal 1966–1996 and the Search for Peace.* Boulder, CO: Roberts Rinehart, 1996.

John V. Denson, ed. — *The Costs of War: America's Pyrrhic Victories.* New Brunswick, NJ: Transaction, 1997.

Paul F. Diehl — *International Peacekeeping.* Rev. ed. Baltimore: Johns Hopkins University Press, 1995.

Barbara Ehrenreich — *Blood Rites: Origins and History of the Passions of War.* New York: Metropolitan Books, 1997.

Daniel William Hallock and Thich Nhat Hanh — *Hell, Healing, and Resistance: Veterans Speak.* Farmington, PA: Plough, 1998.

John Hillen — *Blue Helmets: The Strategy of UN Military Operations.* Washington, DC: Brassey's, 1998.

Richard Holbrooke — *To End a War.* New York: Random House, 1998.

Michael Ignatieff — *The Warrior's Honor: Ethnic War and the Modern Conscience.* New York: Metropolitan Books, 1998.

Donald Kagan — *On the Origin of War and the Preservation of Peace.* New York: Doubleday, 1995.

Fergal Keane — *Season of Blood: A Rwandan Journey.* New York: Viking, 1995.

Yagil Levy — *Trial and Error: Israel's Route from War to De-Escalation.* Albany: State University of New York Press, 1997.

Michael Mandelbaum — *The Dawn of Peace in Europe.* New York: Twentieth Century Fund Press, 1996.

James Mayall, ed. — *The New Interventionism, 1991–1994: United Nations Experience in Cambodia, Former Yugoslavia, and Somalia.* New York: Cambridge University Press, 1996.

Terry Nardin, ed. — *The Ethics of War and Peace: Religious and Secular Perspectives.* Princeton, NJ: Princeton University Press, 1996.

Robert L. Phillips and Duane L. Cady — *Humanitarian Intervention: Just War vs. Pacifism.* Lanham, MD: Rowman & Littlefield, 1996.

David Rieff   *Slaughterhouse: Bosnia and the Failure of the West*. New York: Simon and Schuster, 1995.

Jonathan Stevenson   *We Wrecked the Place: Contemplating an End to the Northern Irish Troubles*. New York: Free Press, 1996.

Charles Townshend, ed.   *The Oxford Illustrated History of Modern War*. New York: Oxford University Press, 1997.

Vamik D. Volkan   *Bloodlines: From Ethnic Pride to Ethnic Terrorism*. New York: Farrar, Strauss, and Giroux, 1997.

Caspar W. Weinberger   *The Next War*. Washington, DC: Regnery, 1996.
and Peter Schweizer

Richard W. Wrangham   *Demonic Males: Apes and the Origins of Human Violence*.
and Dale Peterson   Boston: Houghton Mifflin, 1996.

INDEX